The Authorities

Powerful Wisdom from Leaders in the Field

STEPHEN RICHES
Founder of the Talent CAN Be Taught™ System

©2016 by 10-10-10 Publishing

All rights reserved. No part of this publication may be reproduced or transmitted in any form or by any means, electronic or mechanical, including photocopying, recording, or any other information storage and retrieval system without the written permission of the publisher and author.

Published by:
10-10-10 PUBLISHING
MARKHAM, ON
CANADA

Printed in the United States of America.
ISBN: 978-1-77277-119-0

FOREWORD

Experts are to be admired for their knowledge, but they often remain unrecognized by the general public because they save their information and insights for paying customers and clients. There are many experts in a given field, but their impact is limited to the handful of people with whom they work.

Unlike experts, authorities share their knowledge and expertise far more broadly, so they make a big impact on the world. Authorities become known and admired as leading experts and, as such, typically do very well economically and professionally. Most authorities are also mature enough to know that part of the joy of monetary success is the accompanying moral and spiritual obligation to give back.

Many people want to learn and work with well-respected and generous authorities, but don't always know where to find them. They may be known to their peers, or within a specific community, but have not had the opportunity to reach a wider audience. At one time, they might have submitted a proposal to the For Dummies or Chicken Soup for the Soul series of books, but it's now almost impossible to get accepted as a new author in such branded book series.

It is more than fitting that Raymond Aaron, an internationally known and respected authority in his own right, would be the one to recognize the need for a new venue in which authorities could share their considerable knowledge with readers everywhere. As the only author ever to be included in both of the book series mentioned above, Raymond has had the opportunity to give back and he understands how crucial it is for authorities to have a platform from which to share their expertise.

I have known and worked with Raymond for a number of years and consider him a valued friend and talented coach. He knows how to spot talented and knowledgeable people and he desires to see them prosper. Over the years, success coaching and speaking engagements around the world have made it possible for Raymond to meet many of these talented authorities. He recognizes and relates to their passion and enthusiasm for what they do, as well as their desire to share what they know. He tells me that's why he created this new nonfiction branded book series, *The Authorities*.

Dr. Nido Qubein
President, High Point University

TABLE OF CONTENTS

Introduction V

Achieving a Better Legacy for Private Music Students 1
Stephen Riches

The 3 Things You Need to Become a Real Estate Millionaire 17
Raymond Aaron

Happiness: How to Experience the "Real Deals" 23
Marci Shimoff

Sex, Love and Relationships 33
Dr. John Gray

Family Is Everything 39
Dan Rogers

One Step at a Time 61
Parents, Educators and Children with Autism share their success stories
Anne-Carol Sharples

Declutter Your Mind For Success 75
Erin Muldoon Stetson

Outshine the Competition: Coming Out on Top in the Interview Process . . 89
Ossy Botha

Control Money Before it Controls You 109
K. Raj Singh

Keep Your Job & Get Promoted ...Guaranteed 131
Frantz Forestal

The Vegan Lifestyle Solution 139
Dagmar Schoenrock

Break Through Your Barriers & Live Your Dreams 153
Sandra Westland

INTRODUCTION

This book introduces you to *The Authorities* — individuals who have distinguished themselves in life and in business. Authorities make a big impact on the world. Authorities are leaders in their chosen fields. Authorities typically do very well financially, and are evolved enough to know that part of the joy of monetary success is the accompanying social, moral and spiritual obligation to give back.

Authorities are not just outstanding. They are also *known* to be outstanding.

This additional element begins to explain the difference between two strategic business and life concepts — one that seems great, but isn't, and the other that fills in the essential missing gap of the first.

The first concept is "the expert."

What is an expert? The real definition is …

EXPERT: *a person who knows stuff*

People who have attained a very senior academic degree (like a PhD or an MD) definitely know stuff. People who read voraciously and retain what they read definitely know stuff. Unfortunately, just because you know stuff does not mean that anyone respects the fact that you do. Even though some experts are successful, alas, most are not — because knowing stuff is not enough.

Well, then, what is the missing piece?

What the expert lacks, "the authority" has. The authority both knows stuff and is *known* to know stuff. So, more simply …

AUTHORITY: *a person who is known as an expert*

The difference is not subtle. The difference is not merely semantic. The difference is enormous.

When it comes to this subject, there are actually three categories in which people fall:

- People who don't know much and are unsuccessful in life and in business. Most people fall in this category.

- People who know stuff, but still don't leave much of a footprint in the world. There are a lot of people like this.

- Experts who are also *known* as experts become authorities and authorities are always wondrously successful. Authorities are able to contribute more to humanity through both their chosen work and their giving back.

This book is about the highest category, *The Authorities* — people who have reached the peak in their field and are known as such.

You will definitely know some of *The Authorities* in this book, especially since there are some world-famous ones. Others are just as exceptional, but you may not yet know about them. Our featured author is Stephen Riches. He has created a revolutionary system for private music lessons. In so doing, he has effectively eliminated all of the obstacles that have plagued students for many decades causing the vast majority of all beginners to give up on their dream of ever becoming musically talented. More importantly, he has created a blueprint for the development of music talent that makes becoming talented simply a matter of choice. So if you are considering starting out on your own quest for music talent, be sure to learn how you can eliminate a lot of the biggest challenges right from the start and accelerate your journey to success.

To be considered for inclusion in a subsequent edition of *The Authorities*, register to attend a future event at www.aaron.com/events where you will be interviewed and considered.

VIII

Achieving a Better Legacy for Private Music Students

STEPHEN RICHES

Have you reached a point in your life where you would like to try a new activity or learn a new skill? Why haven't you? If you are like many people, a few failed attempts make you believe that you aren't talented enough to master the skill set, or perhaps you believe you are too old to start. The process gets abandoned and you chalk it up to something that "wasn't meant to be."

The reality is that this does not need to happen. Becoming talented is neither a mysterious nor a daunting process, but rather, like most things in life, simply one that requires a proven successful plan of action. So right now would be a great time for you to change your perception of your own ability.

In my first book, Talent CAN Be Taught: The Book on Creating Music Ability, I debunked the myth that music talent or skill is something that only a few of the elite may enjoy, and introduced the acronym, PRAISE™, which will provide you and students everywhere with an actual blueprint for successfully developing your music skills. Even better, many of these principles may be applied in other areas of your life.

Your ability to achieve can often be wrapped up in how you view yourself. Do you see your skills as the assets that they are, or do you find yourself setting up barriers to your own success? And, with the recent discoveries by neuroscientists that point to the fact that by developing music skills you also greatly improve your brain structure and function, there may be no better way to equip yourself for a lifetime than to invest in yourself with music training.

In this chapter, I will introduce to you the principles that I have used to help my students grow music talent. Some of these, undoubtedly, will seem very logical and straightforward to you. So, if you have ever dreamed of having music talent, don't allow your fears of what others might think to stand in your way. The first step, especially if you ever had lessons in the past but gave up on your dream, is to understand that the reason most students lose interest, become discouraged and quit is because the system failed to ensure that they received the basic training that they needed to succeed.

In fact, private music lessons have presented insurmountable challenges for almost all beginning students for many decades. The problems that arise are the result of the strategies used by most music teachers and teaching studios, rather than with the students themselves, who, unfortunately, are usually blamed for their own lack of success. And, the root cause of the entire problem is one that stems from a general misunderstanding about what talent really is and how talent is created in the first place. So that is where I start my chapter.

UNDERSTANDING TALENT

Many people consider talent to be something that is innate; something that you either have or do not have, and over which you have no control. This is, in large part, due to the ideas that most of us have regarding what talent really is. If we see someone who is very young who displays music ability, we tend to say that this person is very talented. But this begs the question that if someone who is older has developed the very same skills, why should this older person not be considered to be equally talented.

In other words, why should talent simply be considered the domain of those who learn more quickly or at a younger age? Should talent not be evaluated on the basis of skills that can be demonstrated, rather than the age or the speed at which they were acquired? Just as "the proof of the pudding is in the eating", so the evidence of the talent is in the performing, rather than the age of the performer. It is these special music skills or abilities that set talented people apart and which are an indicator of their talent.

A FAILING TRADITION

Whether or not talent can be acquired is something that has been debated for many years. But where there is certainly no doubt is that in the vast majority of cases, beginning students do not become talented. And it is perhaps this fact that has led so many people to assume that their failure to progress well in developing music skills was due to an innate lack of pre-existing talent in the first place. The truth, however, is that millions of people have been victims of a failing tradition in private music education. In my book, Talent CAN Be Taught™, I first identify the signs of this systemic failure, and then present strategies that are providing exciting solutions for my students. This chapter highlights a few of the main points.

The reality is that well over 90% of all students quit private music lessons within a couple of months to a few years and go through the rest of their lives unable to perform any of the pieces that they ever learned, believing that they were responsible for their own lack of success. The causes of this high failure rate rest with critical mistakes and teaching strategies made especially by parents and teachers.

I refer to one of the causes of this failing tradition as the Tom Sawyer School of Learning, after the character in the Mark Twain novel who is able to present documented evidence of achievement without actually ever having done the required work, or acquiring the knowledge that his evidence suggests he has. First of all, he devises a strategy to get paid by his friends so that they can have the privilege of doing the work of whitewashing his aunt's fence, which she had intended to be a punishment for him skipping school the day before. And then he buys Sunday school tickets from his friends the next day by selling their loot back to them in order to receive an honour which he has not earned, in the form of an award given to all those who manage to memorize two thousand Bible verses. In the end, however, the fraud is exposed in front of the entire community, as he is unable to even correctly identify the names of just two of Jesus' disciples.

It is an unfortunate fact, however, that parents, students, and teachers sometimes work together in a way that actually defeats the system, in the same manner as Mark Twain's fictional character does. Due to a quest by parents and students to achieve accreditation as quickly as possible, teachers fail to help students to acquire any of the actual music skills that are the real purpose of the lessons in the first place. Parents and students engage in as few lessons as possible. Teachers skip pages of the curriculum books, books of curriculum levels, entire levels of curricula, and in general then "hopscotch" their way through RCM grades to acquire a Grade 7 and/or Grade 8 RCM certificate for high school credits or to pad their resumes for future career opportunities. Some students have learned as few as a couple of dozen pieces over all of their years of private music training to accomplish this feat. They do not actually learn to read music, nor do they develop the ability to play by ear, which are the two most basic of all music skills. Due to the enormous struggle involved in learning advanced level pieces with undeveloped or under-developed reading skills, even students who manage to survive hate this process so much that they abandon the music they learned forever. As a result, there is a great multitude of students who have achieved Grade 8 level of Royal Conservatory of Music certificates who are unable to play even a single piece of music that they have ever learned.

So, to summarize the problem, some of the most obvious signs of this failing tradition are:

- Inability to remember and perform any music that was ever learned
- Inability to read music at sight beyond a very elementary level, sometimes even Pre-Grade 1
- Inability to learn or play new music by ear
- Deficiencies in technical skill development
- Lack of understanding of musical style

- A more than 90% dropout rate of all beginners every three years

Compounding the problem is that many private music teachers themselves have been the product of this failing tradition. In many cases, not only do they not perform publicly themselves, but they don't even perform for their students, despite the fact that this is the most effective of all teaching strategies. Further, despite their own weaknesses, they have no plans for their own personal professional development. And so, predictably, they continue to use the same failing strategies that led to their own weaknesses and duplicate these shortcomings in their own students.

The Powerful PRAISE Techniques™ explained in detail in my first book called Talent CAN Be Taught: The Book on Creating Music Ability are the key steps which form the blueprint for successfully creating music ability. The word PRAISE is an acronym for these six very important steps to success. Following is a brief synopsis of these key steps.

THE 6 POWERFUL PRAISE TECHNIQUES™

Performance & Repertory – The Core Essence of Music
Why the system begins with performance

Music begins with performance because music is a performance art. If music isn't performed by someone, it doesn't exist. A repertory is a personal collection of music that a particular performer can play at any time by memory.

Results & Accreditation – The Benchmarks of Achievement
The value of certificates and goal setting

While seeking to acquire certificates rather than usable music skills is to put the proverbial cart before the horse, accreditation does have a valuable role to play in measuring student progress. Awards and certificates honour achievement and provide goals for the achievement of excellence. These important measurable, attainable, and most importantly, dated goals for achievement are important steps in the learning process, without which all achievement is jeopardized.

Acceleration & Motivation – The MAGIC of Synergy™
The power of this element in the learning process

One of the reasons that so many students give up on themselves is that they perceive that the learning process is taking too long and they lose interest. Most students, due to poor strategies used by their parents and teachers, never are able to develop any synergy of learning. Acquiring momentum, enjoying accelerated learning, experiencing growth of skills and abilities, feeling inspired to become even better, and being motivated by competition, (either internal or external), to achieve as high a standard of excellence as possible, are all very important steps to success for everyone in all aspects of life. Becoming musically talented is no exception.

Insights & Strategies – The Philosophy of Education
"Only perfect practice makes perfect"

Talent CAN Be Taught presents a number of important insights and strategies for the successful development of music skills. For example, it is a common misconception that practice makes perfect. Student failures, in fact, are often blamed either on a lack of talent or a lack of practice, both of which fail to recognize the real cause of the failures. This famous and often misquoted Vince Lombardi gem is one example of a philosophy or insight that is presented in the book. What the legendary football coach actually said was that "perfect practice makes perfect". However, the reality is that beginners do not know how to practice, and bad practice never achieves good results. In fact, practicing independently usually leads to frustration for almost all beginners. All students need to be first taught how to practice rather than just what to practice. And students should only be asked to practice after they have been well-prepared for independent learning. This necessarily includes having some basic reading and ear training skills. Most beginners, however, are too young to understand and use sound pedagogical strategies for independent learning. As a result, independent practice often causes more harm than good in the beginning stages of training. In the early stages, practice needs to be monitored by an expert.

Supervision & Curriculum – The Tools of Training
The role of teachers and teaching materials

Private independent teachers, by definition, have no supervisory support. Nor do many follow a curriculum in its entirety to ensure that all concepts are taught. Many or most parents either do not understand or perhaps underestimate the value or importance of the role that supervision and curriculum have to play in a student's training even though it is taken for granted in public education. The music skills that we recognize as indicators of talent do not happen by accident or over time by independent practice alone. Like all skills in all vocations, they must be taught by an expert. An important part of the TCBT system is in making sure that our teachers are equipped to provide the most expert training possible for the students. This philosophy is at the core of all that has led to the great successes of our unique Talent CAN Be Taught™ system.

The most important factor in education for all teachers and students is the need for an outstanding comprehensive and sequential curriculum. Many curricula have weaknesses in the sequence or order that concepts are taught, the size of the challenges presented to the students, and in maintaining consistently small and attainable and progressive steps for learning. These shortcomings always contribute to frustration. However, the TCBT system follows what we consider to be the very best curriculum available, which we mandate to be used by all of our teachers and students. This is also discussed in some detail in the book.

Why is using a good curriculum so important? Well, first of all, teachers are able to follow it as a daybook to systematically track the lessons that they provide. And, students who follow it are able to avoid developing gaps in their music education that always cause the learning experience to become slower, more frustrating, and less enjoyable with every level of advancement. The irony is that the shortcuts that are often taken in the quest for faster advancement and achieving higher certificates at an earlier date actually slow down the learning process. By contrast, with the TCBT system, student skill development is occurring so rapidly that some of the students have progressed from Grade 1 to Grade 6 in only two years without skipping any grade levels or exams, and have achieved First Class Honours on their exams at every level while learning hundreds of pieces of music during that time.

Ear Training & Reading Skills – The Basic Fundamentals
"Do you play by ear, or do you read music?"

As a young person, I often had an opportunity to perform for recitals or other occasions or special events. Invariably, people would see me perform by memory and ask whether I read music or played by ear. My answer, of course, was "both". At the time, I had no idea how profound this response was. For what other method is there? Either you play by ear, or you read music, and ideally both, for these are the two fundamentally basic of all music skills. And yet, both of these important skills are among the common denominators that are missing for the vast majority of students who quit taking lessons after just a few months or years. They quit because they cannot read music, nor can they play by ear, and so they find it frustrating trying to learn mainly by rote and are not enjoying it. The Talent CAN Be Taught™ system ensures that ear and reading skills are actually taught, and these vital and basic fundamentals which are taught at every step of the way complete the six Powerful PRAISE Techniques™ that contribute to the great success of the students.

The Achievers Programs™
The success of the pilot program

The Achievers Programs™ were developed to ensure student success in keeping with the principles outlined in the six Powerful PRAISE Techniques™ that make up the core part of the TCBT system. The inspiration that led to the development of these accelerated learning programs resulted from the experience of one particular student and the strategy that I implemented as a pilot program for him. This student had chosen to begin taking a trial month of guitar lessons. He could not read music, and did not know how to practice, and had become frustrated very quickly trying to practice independently six days a week. Within two weeks, he had lost interest and stopped practicing. So we made a switch. Instead of guitar, we gave him a fresh start on piano. I made a deal with him that he didn't have to practice, in order to eliminate the tension at home that had occurred due to his Mom's insistence that he had to practice every day. We gave him three half-hour lessons per week instead of one, and I reduced the price per lesson as an incentive to invest more overall to the strategy. Of course, we also used the outstanding house piano/keyboard curriculum. There were, and still are today, five main goals of this program as follows:

- provide more frequent, regular, expert teacher support

- reduce per-lesson cost to encourage parents to make a larger short-term financial commitment

- enhance foundational learning with a switch to piano training

- eliminate the source of tension and liabilities associated with forced independent practice

- to create synergy among the various learning components with the frequency of instruction

Less than three months after starting this pilot program, I discovered that the student, who had been working with another teacher at my studio, was beginning the fifth level in the curriculum. And this curriculum had 4 books at each level. His mother had this explanation for how he had managed to go through 16 curriculum books in just 10 weeks:

"Oh, I forgot to tell you. He won't stop practicing. He practices at all hours during the day, even first thing in the morning before school. I put an alarm clock on the piano set for 8:15 AM. I tell him that when the alarm goes off, he has to stop playing the piano and go to school, or he is going to be late. I may be upstairs vacuuming and hear the alarm go off. I turn off the vacuum cleaner to listen, and the sounds from the piano keep on going. So I have to come downstairs to physically remove him from the piano bench and send him off to school."

So what happened here? Well, this student, who had previously very quickly become disinterested in the instrument of his choice (guitar), was now thriving on piano as a result of the implementation of the Powerful PRAISE Techniques™ that form the core principles of the TCBT system. I immediately began to promote these strategies for all of our students. Within three years, all of the students who participated in the program were able to accelerate through as many as eight levels of study achieving excellence at every level.

BUILDING A NEW LEGACY FOR THE FUTURE

An Innovative Teacher Apprentice Program

The best of systems can only reach its ultimate achievement when it is duplicated. That, of course is the principle behind the great successes of franchising. And just as many teachers are duplicating their own weaknesses in their students and thereby contributing to the continuation of the failing traditions, so the TCBT teacher apprentice program has been designed to continue and duplicate a new and better system of private music education. This program is designed especially for high school age students who have achieved RCM First Class Honours in Grade 5 Piano and Basic Theory. Students who have not yet achieved this standard of excellence, but who are currently studying at this level may also be admitted to the program. In the apprentice program, students are provided with an opportunity to first improve the quality of their own learning through examination of teaching practices and study of curriculum materials, to earn community service credits for high school by assisting beginning students, and eventually to earn part-time income through teaching beginning level students themselves. Those who progress to the highest levels of achievement will have an opportunity to become leaders of the Talent CAN Be Taught™ system to continue the legacy for future generations.

While piano/keyboard training is the best foundation for all music studies, the principles, of course, are transferable to other instruments and voice. At TCBT studios, we encourage many students to diversify and take a second instrument when they are ready for the additional experience. Some may receive this supplemental training in the public education system, but many do not. And all benefit greatly from receiving supplemental expert support with their band or orchestra instrument that isn't available in the context of a music classroom setting. Without exception, these students become the leaders in their school music programs.

AN AFTERWORD TO THE CHAPTER

In Talent CAN Be Taught; The Book on Creating Music Ability, I drew attention to the shortcuts that students were taking, and the resulting mine field that causes almost all private music students to get frustrated and give up on themselves within a few months to a few years. They incorrectly assumed, or in some cases were perhaps even told that the reason that they were not progressing was because they lacked talent, when, in fact, the real reason was due to historically ineffective teaching routines and strategies, and especially the ill-advised shortcuts that have been used by parents, teachers, and students for many years. These are explained in detail in the book, along with numerous recommended solutions.

In this single chapter, therefore, I have merely summarized and highlighted some of the key points of the book, while necessarily leaving out an explanation of most of the important details.

So while I hope that you found this chapter helpful as an introduction to the topic of how to ensure quality results with private music lessons, I encourage anyone who is serious about developing music skills to read the entire book.

In summary, the book includes a detailed explanation of many of the most common errors made by parents, students, and private teachers engaged in private music education. It also includes a diagnostic survey that will help readers to recognize if they have been a victim themselves of what I refer to as the failing traditions. Finally, it provides the proven blueprint for success through a detailed explanation of the role of The Powerful PRAISE Techniques™, as well as a number of helpful insights and strategies for success. These are critically important for all students of any age who would like to have great music skills, even for those who had previously given up on their own personal quest for talent, and who may now be inspired to renew their efforts buoyed by a better understanding of the proven keys to success.

TESTIMONIALS

"Stephen's vision and commitment to achieving a better future for private music education is truly inspiring. His passion for excellence, which I have been privileged to observe firsthand, is evident in his book's reflections and challenge for future engagement."

Reg Andrews
Administrator, Pickering Christian Academy, (Markham, ON)
www.pca.ca

"If your child is now or soon will be taking piano lessons, you need to read this book, because all students deserve to have teachers who really understand and value the important lessons this book contains."

Frank Feather
global business futurist, author, and father to two pianist daughters (Aurora, ON)
www.ffeather.com

"I took piano lessons for 9 years as a child and today, I cannot play anything! I thought that was because I was not naturally talented. If I had understood the concepts in this book – that talent can be taught – today I would be a professional piano player, entertaining people around the world!"

Dr. Robert A. Rohm Ph.D
speaker, author (Atlanta, GA)
www.personalityinsights.com

"I first met Stephen around the time he published his first book. I was so impressed with his commitment to making changes to improve how music is taught for the benefit of students everywhere that I invited him to be co-author of my second volume of *The Road to Success*"

Jack Canfield
entrepreneur, success coach, and co-author of the
Chicken Soup for the Soul books (Santa Barbara, CA)
www.jackcanfield.com

The 3 Things You Need to Become a Real Estate Millionaire

The Right Way to Invest Successfully

RAYMOND AARON

It seems like everywhere you look, someone is claiming that they became a millionaire by investing in real estate, and encouraging you to do the same. There are lots of TV shows about flipping houses for a fast buck that make it appear as if it's easy to find the right property and just as easy to sell it in a matter of months for a good profit. Unfortunately, that's not really how it works.

Investing in real estate is a proven way to make money, a lot of it. You could end up with millions, but you could also make a lot of very costly mistakes along the way. There has been so much hype about how easy it is to become a real estate millionaire that many people jump into the market without knowing what they are doing, and that's a shame, especially because qualified help is available.

Anyone can invest successfully in real estate if they have three things: a great real estate mentor, a proven real estate system, and a way to correctly predict the future. In other words, you need someone smart and knowledgeable to guide you, an understanding of the financial and legal aspects of buying, holding and selling real estate, and an ability to see societal trends and visualize how those trends will impact the real estate market.

A GREAT REAL ESTATE MENTOR

Investing on your own can be financially dangerous, especially for a first-timer. You're dealing with a lot of money, so any mistake can be a huge one. Buying at the wrong time in the cycle can kill your investments. And, regardless of the real estate strategy you employ, you're bound to hold onto properties for some period of time which means that severe negative cash flow and vacancies can ruin you. Plus, bad property management and a failure to know the most recent real estate and tax laws can get you sued.

An experienced mentor can help you choose the best real estate strategies for your situation, and the right properties in which to invest. They can also help you avoid the many possible pitfalls and make money while holding properties, and counsel you on when to sell for a great profit. Working with the right mentor can also keep real estate investing from becoming your full-time job.

Many people find that some part of the investment process is uncomfortable for them, whether it's initiating a conversation with a realtor, submitting an offer or hiring a property manager. A mentor can be very helpful in such situations as well.

In sum, learning from and working with the right mentor can make you a highly profitable investor in a relatively short period of time. Look for someone with years of experience and a proven track record.

A PROVEN SYSTEM

There's much more to investing in real estate than "buy low, sell high." To be successful, you must have the correct facts and the correct monthly habits concerning your real estate. Overall, you need to know what to buy, when to buy it, whether there will be a positive cash flow while you're holding on to it, and when to sell. Plus, what is the right low? What is the right high? How much money do you have to put down and how much income must be generated while you're waiting to sell?

Determining if a property is a good buy takes a lot of research and analysis. You will need to look at comparable purchase prices in the area, as well as rental fees. You'll also need to consider the location, the age and condition of the building, tax rates and about 30 other pieces of data. Evaluating the information for just one property could take you a day or more.

If you're serious about becoming a real estate investor, you are going to be considering quite a lot of properties on a regular basis. Even if you want to make investing your day job, you'll never have the time necessary to research fully and evaluate every property that comes to your attention. Hence, the first part of your system has to involve weeding out the lesser opportunities and focusing on the ones with potential.

The investors I mentor learn how to determine if a property is really a great deal in seconds. You only need two pieces of data: the purchase price and the current rent rate. Compare the two using a two-part formula. First, divide the asking price (outgoing funds) by 100. Then, given that current mortgage interest rates are below 8-10% divide the number you got by two. If the current monthly rent doesn't meet or better that second number, eliminate the property from consideration.

As an example, say the asking price is $1 million. If you divide it by 100, it comes out to $10 thousand. Divide again, by two, and you get $5 thousand. If the monthly rent isn't $5 thousand or more, you should pass on the property. You may miss out on a few winners using this system but, if you eliminate more properties than you think you should, you'll be successful and safe. Remember that, if interest rates rise significantly, you will need to adjust the formula to compensate.

Once you've weeded out the chaff from the wheat, do your due diligence on the remaining properties. Work closely with your mentor during this part of the process and, again, when it comes to making deals, say no more than you say yes. Just don't get cold feet or shy away from a great deal.

In terms of timing, it all comes down to momentum. There is always an overall upward momentum. Real estate prices go up and down, on an upwards track. So, one good profit strategy is to buy low, watch values rise and sell during the next boom. More precisely, you want to buy just as prices rise off the bottom (so that they're already rising) and sell when prices hit double the bottom, which is typically the very minimum prices rise to at the peak of the ensuing boom.

Don't attempt to predict the extremes — you will make a significant amount of money more safely buying just after prices begin rising (not the lowest point) and selling towards the end of the up period —without the risk associated with waiting too long and missing the highest point.

You'll also need a system for monitoring your investments while holding on until it's time to sell. Having a strong property manager is essential. So is reviewing rents taken in versus uncollectibles, repairs, and other expenses to ensure that your cash flow remains positive.

PREDICTING THE FUTURE

Good real estate investors learn to identify marketplace trends and buyers' or renters' needs. Start by investigating and tracking growth trends by neighborhood: are prices rising, is an area getting ready for a renaissance, are there new job opportunities nearby or is the area close to another neighborhood that's gotten too pricey?

Great real estate investors, however, go far beyond those basics. They look for large demographic or social elements that might provide the next big opportunity. The huge number of returning veterans after World War II led to a Baby Boom that provides the perfect example. Every stage of their lives brought an opportunity for marketers, real estate builders, and other manufacturers to fill unmet needs, be it starter homes for when they had children, tricycles for those children who were too young to ride a bike, or new sizes and types of cars. All of this was predictable, but no one noticed. Opportunities were capitalized upon as they arose, but imagine what financial success could have been attained if someone had predicted the Baby Boomers' needs in advance.

And, now, those Boomers are driving the growth of retirement communities and nursing homes. But, they are a more independent lot than their parents were, and have strived to remain young and healthy as long as possible. Quite a few of them can still live and thrive on their own, but many may need a little help at this point in their lives. They don't need or want an aide, nurse or social worker on a full-time basis and certainly aren't ready for a nursing home. That means there is a huge need for more up-to-date, internet-ready independent supportive living arrangements, of which there are too few. Investing in one now is bound to be a win.

Don't forget that those Baby Boomers had children of their own, and that created a mini baby boom. Think about the ways in which those children, now middle-aged adults, are different from their parents and what needs they might have, especially regarding real estate. You might also consider whether changes in the workforce, higher divorce rates and the economics of leaving home after college have implications for the real estate market as well. Keep your eyes and minds open!

If you would like to learn more about winning strategies for investing in real estate, please visit http://rarestmonthlymentor.com.

Happiness: How to Experience the "Real Deals"

MARCI SHIMOFF

I was 41 years old, stretched out on a lounge chair by my pool and reflecting on my life. I had achieved all that I thought I needed to be happy.

You see, when I was a child, I thought there would be five main things that would ensure that I'd be happy: a successful career helping people, a loving husband, a comfortable home, a great body, and a wonderful circle of friends. After years of study, hard work, and a few "lucky breaks," I finally had them all. (Okay, so my body didn't quite look like Halle Berry's—but four out of five isn't bad!) You think I'd have been on the top of the world.

But surprisingly I wasn't. I felt an emptiness inside that the outer successes of life couldn't fill. I was also afraid that if I lost any of those things, I might be miserable. Sadly, I knew I wasn't alone in feeling this way.

While happiness is the one thing we all truly want, so few people really experience the deep and lasting fulfillment that fills our soul. Why aren't we finding it?

Because, in the words of the old country western song, we're looking for happiness in "all the wrong places."

Looking around, I saw that the happiest people I knew weren't the most successful and famous. Some were married, some were single. Some had lots of money, and some didn't have a dime. Some of them even had health challenges. From where I stood, there seemed to be no rhyme or reason to what made people happy. The obvious question became: *Could a person actually be happy for no reason?*

I had to find out.

So I threw myself into the study of happiness. I interviewed scores of scientists, as well as 100 unconditionally happy people. (I call them the Happy 100.) I delved into the research from the burgeoning field of positive psychology, the study of the positive traits that enable people to enjoy meaningful, fulfilling, and happy lives.

What I found changed my life. To share this knowledge with others, I wrote a book called *Happy for No Reason: 7 Steps to Being Happy from the Inside Out*.

One day, as I sat down to compile my findings, all the pieces of the puzzle fell into place. I had a simple, but profound "a-ha"—there's a continuum of happiness:

Unhappy: We all know what this means: life seems flat. Some of the signs are anxiety, fatigue, feeling blue or low—your "garden-variety" unhappiness. This isn't the same as clinical depression, which is characterized by deep despair and hopelessness that dramatically interferes with your ability to live a normal life, and for which professional help is absolutely necessary.

Happy for Bad Reason: When people are unhappy, they often try to make themselves feel better by indulging in addictions or behaviors that may feel good in the moment but are ultimately detrimental. They seek the highs that come from drugs, alcohol, excessive sex, "retail therapy," compulsive gambling, over-eating, and too much television-watching, to name a few. This kind of "happiness" is hardly happiness at all. It is only a temporary way to numb or escape our unhappiness through fleeting experiences of pleasure.

Happy for Good Reason: This is what people usually mean by happiness: having good relationships with our family and friends, success in our careers, financial security, a nice house or car, or using our talents and strengths well. It's the pleasure we derive from having the healthy things in our lives that we want.

Don't get me wrong. I'm all for this kind of happiness! It's just that it's only half the story. Being Happy for Good Reason depends on the external conditions of our lives—these conditions change or are lost, our happiness usually goes too. Relying solely on this type of happiness is where a lot of our fear is stemming from these days. We're afraid the things we think we need to be happy may be slipping from our grasp.

Deep inside, I think we all know that life isn't meant to be about getting by, numbing our pain, or having everything "under control." True happiness doesn't come from merely collecting an assortment of happy experiences. At our core, we know there's something more than this.

There is. It's the next level on the happiness continuum—Happy for No Reason.

Happy for No Reason: This is true happiness—a state of peace and well-being that isn't dependent on external circumstances.

Happy for No Reason isn't elation, euphoria, mood spikes, or peak experiences that don't last. It doesn't mean grinning like a fool 24/7 or experiencing a superficial high. Happy for No Reason isn't an emotion. In fact, when you are Happy for No Reason, you can have *any* emotion—including sadness, fear, anger or hurt—but you still experience that underlying state of peace and well-being.

When you're Happy for No Reason, you *bring* happiness to your outer experiences rather than trying to *extract* happiness from them. You don't need to manipulate the world around you to try to make yourself happy. You live from happiness, rather than *for* happiness.

This is a revolutionary concept. Most of us focus on being Happy for Good Reason, stringing together as many happy experiences as we can, like beads in a necklace, to create a happy life. We have to spend a lot of time and energy trying to find just the right beads so we can have a "happy necklace".

Being Happy for No Reason, in our necklace analogy, is like having a happy string. No matter what beads we put on our necklace—good, bad or indifferent—our inner experience, which is the string that runs through them all, is happy, and creates a happy life.

Happy for No Reason is a state that's been spoken of in virtually all spiritual and religious traditions throughout history. The concept is universal. In Buddhism, it is called causeless joy; in Christianity, the kingdom of Heaven within; and in Judaism it is called *ashrei*, an inner sense of holiness and health. In Islam it is called *falah*, happiness and well-being; and in Hinduism it is called *ananda*, or pure bliss. Some traditions refer to it as an enlightened or awakened state.

So how can you be Happy for No Reason?

Science is verifying the way. Researchers in the field of positive psychology have found that we each have a "happiness set-point," that determines our level of happiness. No matter what happens, whether it's something as exhilarating as winning the lottery or as challenging as a horrible accident, most people eventually return to their original happiness level. Like your weight set-point, which keeps the scale hovering around the same number, your happiness set-point will remain the same **unless you make a concerted effort to change it.** In the same way you'd crank up the thermostat to get comfortable on a chilly day, you actually have the power to reprogram your happiness set-point to a higher level of peace and well-being. The secret lies in practicing the habits of happiness.

Some books and programs will tell you that you can simply decide to be happy. They say just make up your mind to be happy—and you will be.

I don't agree.

You can't just decide to be happy, any more than you can decide to be fit or to be a great piano virtuoso and expect instant mastery. You can, however, decide to take the necessary steps, like exercising or taking piano lessons—and by practicing those skills, you can get in shape or give recitals. In the same way, you can become Happy for No Reason through practicing the habits of happy people.

All of your habitual thoughts and behaviors in the past have created specific neural pathways in the wiring in your brain, like grooves in a record. When we think or behave a certain way over and over, the neural pathway is strengthened and the groove becomes deeper—the way a well-traveled route through a field eventually becomes a clear-cut path. Unhappy people tend to have more negative neural pathways. This is why you can't just ignore the realities of your brain's wiring and *decide* to be happy! To raise your level of happiness, you have to create new grooves.

Scientists used to think that once a person reached adulthood, the brain was fairly well "set in stone" and there wasn't much you could do to change it. But new research is revealing exciting information about the brain's neuroplasticity: when you think, feel and act in different ways, the brain changes and actually rewires itself. You aren't doomed to the same negative neural pathways for your whole life. Leading brain researcher Dr. Richard Davidson, of the University of Wisconsin says, "Based on what we know of the plasticity of the brain, we can think of things like happiness and compassion as skills that are no different from learning to play a musical instrument or tennis .... it is possible to train our brains to be happy."

While a few of the Happy 100 I interviewed were born happy, most of them learned to be happy by practicing habits that supported their happiness. That means wherever you are on the happiness continuum, it's entirely in your power to raise your happiness level.

In the course of my research, I uncovered 21 core happiness habits that anyone can use to become happier and stay that way. You can find all 21 happiness habits at www.HappyForNoReason.com

Here are a few tips to get you started:

1. **Incline Your Mind Toward Joy.** Have you noticed that your mind tends to register the negative events in your life more than the positive? If you get ten compliments in a day and one criticism, what do you remember? For most people, it's the criticism. Scientists call this our "negativity bias" — our primitive survival wiring that causes us to pay more attention to the negative than the positive. To reverse this bias, get into the daily habit of consciously registering the positive around you: the sun on your skin, the taste of a favorite food, a smile or kind word from a co-worker or friend. Once you notice something positive, take a moment to savor it deeply and feel it; make it more than just a mental observation. Spend 20 seconds soaking up the happiness you feel.

2. **Let Love Lead.** One way to power up your heart's flow is by sending loving kindness to your friends and family, as well as strangers you pass on the street. Next time you're waiting for the elevator at work, stuck in a line at the store or caught up in traffic, send a silent wish to the people you see for their happiness, well-being, and health. Simply wishing others well switches on the "pump" in your own heart that generates love and creates a strong current of happiness.

3. **Lighten Your Load.** To make a habit of letting go of worries and negative thoughts, start by letting go on the physical level. Cultural anthropologist Angeles Arrien recommends giving or throwing away 27 items a day for nine days. This deceptively simple practice will help you break attachments that no longer serve you.

4. **Make Your Cells Happy.** Your brain contains a veritable pharmacopeia of natural happiness-enhancing neurochemicals — endorphins, serotonin, oxytocin, and dopamine — just waiting to be released to every organ and cell in your body. The way that you eat, move, rest, and even your facial expression can shift the balance of your body's feel-good-chemicals, or "Joy Juice", in your favor. To dispense some extra Joy Juice — smile. Scientists have discovered that smiling decreases stress hormones and boosts happiness chemicals, which increase the body's T-cells, reduce pain, and enhance relaxation. You may not feel like it, but smiling — even artificially to begin with — starts the ball rolling and will turn into a real smile in short order.

5. **Hang with the Happy.** We catch the emotions of those around us just like we catch their colds — it's called emotional contagion. So it's important to make wise choices about the company you keep. Create appropriate boundaries with emotional bullies and "happiness vampires" who suck the life out of you. Develop your happiness "dream team" — a mastermind or support group you meet with regularly to keep you steady on the path of raising your happiness.

"Happily ever after" isn't just for fairytales or for only the lucky few. Imagine experiencing inner peace and well-being as the backdrop for everything else in your life. When you're Happy for No Reason, it's not that your life always looks perfect — it's that, however it looks, you'll still be happy!

By Marci Shimoff. Based on the New York Times bestseller *Happy for No Reason: 7 Steps to Being Happy from the Inside Out*, which offers a revolutionary approach to experiencing deep and lasting happiness. The woman's face of the *Chicken Soup for the Soul* series and a featured teacher in *The Secret*, Marci is an authority on success, happiness, and the law of attraction. To order *Happy for No Reason* and receive free bonus gifts, go to www.happyfornoreason.com/mybook.

Sex, Love and Relationships

DR. JOHN GRAY

Just as great sex is important to lasting love, good health is important to sex and relationships. About 12 years ago, I cured myself of early stage Parkinson's disease. The doctors were amazed, but my wife was even more amazed. She noted that our relationship and sex life had become dramatically better. It turns out that the natural supplements I used to reverse Parkinson's can also make you more attentive and loving in your relationship. At that point, I realized that good relationship skills alone were not enough to sustain love and passion for a lifetime.

I shared many insights gained from my 40 years' experience as a marriage counselor and coach in *Men Are From Mars, Women Are From Venus*. And while my insights go a long way towards helping men and women understand and support each other, good communication skills alone are not always enough. For better relationships, we not only need to be healthy, but we must also experience optimum brain function.

If you are tired, depressed, anxious, not sleeping well, or in pain, then certainly romantic feelings will become a thing of the past. My recovery from Parkinson's revealed to me the profound connection between the quality of our health and our relationships. This insight has motivated me, over the past twelve years, to research the secrets of optimum health as a foundation for lasting love.

These are health secrets that are generally not explored in medical school. In medical school, doctors are indoctrinated into the culture of examining the symptoms, identifying the sickness, and prescribing a drug to treat that sickness. They learn very little about how to be healthy or to sustain successful relationships.

There are no university courses entitled "Better Nutrition For Better Sex". Drugs sometimes save lives, but they also have negative side effects that do little to preserve the passion in a relationship. Ideally, drugs should be used as a last resort and 90 % of our health plan should be drug free. From this perspective, the heath care crisis, as well as our high rate of divorce in America, is indirectly caused by our dependence on doctors and prescription drugs.

Most people have not even considered that taking prescribed drugs (even for the small stuff) can weaken their relationships, which in turn makes them more vulnerable to more disease. For example, if you are feeling depressed or anxious, a drug may numb your pain, but it does nothing to help you correct the cause of your problem. It can even prevent you from feeling your natural motivation to get the emotional support you need. In a variety of ways, our common health complaints are all expressions of two major conditions: our lack of education to identify and support unmet gender-specific emotional needs; and our lack of education to identify and support unmet gender-specific nutritional needs.

With an understanding of natural solutions that have been around for thousands of years, drugs are not needed to treat many common complaints. Some symptoms like low energy, weight gain, allergies, hormonal imbalance, mood swings, poor sleep, indigestion, lack of focus, ADD and ADHD, procrastination, low motivation, memory loss, decreased libido, PMS, vaginal dryness, muscle and joint pain, or the lack of passion in life and/or our relationships can be treated drug-free. By using drugs (even over-the-counter drugs) to treat these common complaints, our bodies and relationships are weakened, making us more vulnerable to bigger and more costly health challenges like cancer, diabetes, heart disease, auto-immune disease, dementia, and Alzheimer's. In simple terms, by handling the easy stuff (the common complaints) without doctors and drugs, we can protect ourselves from the big stuff (cancer, heart disease, dementia, etc.) We can be healthy and also enjoy lasting love and passion in our personal lives.

Even if you are taking anti-depressants or hormone replacement therapy, sometimes all it takes to stop treating the symptom is to directly handle the cause. With specific mineral orotates (something most people have never heard of) or omega three oil from the brains of salmon, your stress levels immediately drop and you begin to feel happy and in love again.

For every health challenge, we have explored the effects on our relationships, with as well as natural remedies that can sometimes produce immediate positive results. You can find these natural solutions to common health complaints for free at my website: www.MarsVenus.com.

What they don't teach in medical school is how to be healthy and happy without the use of drugs or hormone replacement. By refusing drugs and taking responsibility for your health, a wealth of new possibilities can become available to you. We are designed to be healthy and happy, and it is within our reach if we commit to increasing our knowledge.

New research regarding the brain differences in men and women reveals how specific nutritional supplements, combined with gender-specific relationship and self-nurturing skills, can stimulate the hormones of health, happiness and increased energy. Over the past 10 years in my healing center in California, I witnessed how natural solutions coupled with gender-specific relationship skills could solve our common health complaints without drugs. By addressing these common complaints without prescribed drugs, not only do we feel better, but our relationships have the potential to improve dramatically.

Ultimately the cause of all our common complaints is higher stress levels. Researchers around the world all agree that chronic stress levels in our bodies provide a basis for any and all disease to take hold. An easy and quick solution for lowering our stress reactions is specific nutritional support combined with gender-smart relationship skills. Extra nutritional support is needed because stress depletes the body very quickly of essential nutrients. When a car engine is running more quickly, it uses fuel more quickly. When we are stressed, we need both extra nutrients and extra emotional support. Understanding what we need to take and where to get it requires education. Every week day at www.MarsVenus.com I have a live daily show where I freely answer questions and provide this much-needed new gender-specific insight.

At www.MarsVenus.com, we are happy to share what we have learned for creating healthy bodies and positive relationships. You can find a host of natural solutions for common complaints and feel confident that you have the power to feel fully alive with an abundance of energy and positive feelings that will enrich all your relationships.

Family Is Everything

DAN ROGERS

Hundreds of years ago wooden ships brought immigrants to the shores of what would become the maritime provinces of Canada. Why did the pioneers brave starvation, malnutrition, disease or shipwreck?

Today, a number of immigrants arrived at Pearson International Airport in Toronto, Ontario. Why did they leave their countries, their jobs and friends to try and carve out a new life in Canada?

Ask such questions of either group and you would likely receive the identical answer: "To build a better life for my family," they would say. Why? Because family is everything!

In 1916 a young couple, Clarence and Lizzy, got married and boarded a train to northwest Saskatchewan. The rules were that if you were over eighteen, married and agreed to live on and work the land, the government would grant you a quarter section, which is 160 acres or 65 hectares.

At first they plowed the virgin fields with a team of oxen. The prairie grass roots were so thick that the girl had to follow along behind the plow, cutting the roots of the prairie grass with a butcher knife. Her first three babies miscarried. Then, on her fourth pregnancy, the boy rounded up just enough money for one train ticket to the closest town that had a hospital (Lloydminster). He took her in a horse drawn wagon across the prairie for many kilometers to the train station, put her on the train and returned home to continue working the fields. The girl gave birth to a healthy baby girl named Grace. That baby girl was my mother.

My grandmother was what was known as a Bernardo child. She was in a program based out of England that was founded by a man named Bernardo. Orphans and children whose parents could not afford to look after them were shipped to Canada to live on farms. Some of the families treated the child as one of their own, while others treated the child as a slave. The end result, however, was that they got to Canada. And it worked, albeit slowly. So … my mother had a better life than her mother … I am having a better life than my mother … and my son, an only child, came home from the hospital not only to his own bedroom, but to one that had a four piece en suite bathroom. Also, by the time my wife and I are gone from this world, he will be an automatic millionaire.

My hope is that you and your family can accomplish this quicker than we did. We were slow learners. It took us over a century to create wealth. But the fact that you are in Canada and reading this book already puts you in the group that is most likely to succeed. Do you find that hard to believe? Then just think of all the people who came home from work today and are either checking Facebook or watching reality TV. They definitely aren't reading a book about how to succeed financially.

THE PURPOSE OF THIS CHAPTER

The purpose of this chapter is to help educate you to use whatever money you have to benefit you and your family in the long run.

The first thing I want to do is ask you a question: What is your biggest asset? Many people will answer that question by stating what they own. Various answers will be the most obvious ones like my house, my car, my life insurance policy, my retirement fund. But the real answer is you or, to be more accurate, it's your ability to earn a living.

Now, consider that the average annual income in Canada is around fifty thousand dollars (at time of printing). That means in a typical forty year career you will have grossed two million dollars. Yet, most Canadians don't own two million dollars of mortgage free real estate or don't have two million dollars in the bank or even in an insurance policy. Why is that?

It's simple mathematics ...

Mr. A and Mr. B both moved to Canada about fifty years ago from the same country. They both got jobs at the same company for the same wage. But Mr. A saved up his money for a down payment on a house and also budgeted in the monthly premium for a permanent life insurance policy, while Mr. B spent much of his disposable income on trips back to his homeland, coffee shops, take- out food, and cigarettes.

Both A and B died about twenty years ago. The daughter of Mr. A inherited a mortgage free house and a life insurance policy, while the son of Mr. B ended up with nothing. Because the child of A immediately had cash in hand, from the insurance money, and she chose to live in the house for free, she was able to invest both the life insurance money and the monthly rent she had previously been paying. Meanwhile, the son of Mr. B had to save for years and years before he could get out of the apartment he was renting, because saving up while paying rent is much more challenging. In the end, however, B descendent was able to buy a house and make some modest investments.

Eventually the heirs of both Mr. A and Mr. B died. The grandchildren of A have inherited multiple real estate properties and investment funds easily worth in excess of a million dollars, while the family of Mr. B ended up with only a few hundred thousand, as the real estate and other investments were purchased later in their parents' lives and didn't have time enough to grow. The property may not have even been mortgage free at the time of Mr. B's death.

So, the third generation of the A family are now millionaires, while the same generation of the B family has enough money for a modest down payment on a nice house.

You want to be Mr or Mrs A. Buy a home early and pay off that mortgage. Protect your ability to earn with the proper insurance policies and invest on an ongoing basis. Read on, I'll show you how to do it. But first a discussion about estate planning

WILL AND POWER OF ATTORNEY

We have been talking about estates. These are passed on to beneficiaries through the vehicle known as the will. But, over the several years that I have been in this profession, I have encountered a rather high percentage of people that do not have their wills done. And you do need one. Not a "do it yourself" will kit that can be purchased online or at a business supply retailer. Generally, the legal system does not consider this type of will to be valid. No, I strongly urge you to have a lawyer draw up your will. A good lawyer. A conscientious lawyer. Here's why …

An elderly widower sells his house, puts the money in the bank, moves to an apartment, and marries a much younger new wife. His lawyer draws up a will stating that his estate will be divided amongst his wife, his three children and his two favourite charities. The lawyer did not enquire about what type of account the money was in or ask any questions of that nature. When the man died, the executor of the estate found out that the bank had advised the man to name a beneficiary to the account, so the man, not being given a full legal explanation of the ramifications, named his wife as beneficiary. So, on his death, the bank immediately transferred 100% of the funds into the wife's name, and there was no legal recourse to get her to divide up the money according to the will. The will became a useless piece of paper. The three children and the two charities received nothing from the fund. That man was my father.

The lesson to be learned is to never assume that a professional you hire is automatically going to do things in your best interest.

Power of Attorney: There are two types of power of attorney: one for personal care, and one for property. This means that you designate a person to make decisions on your behalf should you reach the point where you can no longer make these decisions yourself. **Personal care** refers to topics such as choosing a personal support worker, a nursing home, treatments, medications, and other things of that nature. **Property** refers to topics such as whether or not to sell the house or rent it out or authorize repairs, and whether to sell the car, or cut the lawn or many other property related items.

In listing a power of attorney, remember that you do not have to have the same person for all areas. You could have a daughter who would be the best for personal care, an eldest son who would make the best executor, and a youngest son who is in real estate who would be the best person for property decisions.

I should also mention **Probate** as it is a complicated and frequently costly procedure wherein you must prove the validity of the will. The general rule is that if there is a beneficiary listed on the account, then probate is not required.

When the funds are in a bank, the money could be in one of several different types of accounts. It could be in a chequing account, a savings account, a TFSA (tax free savings account), an RRSP (registered retirement savings plan), mutual funds, segregated funds, GIC (guaranteed investment certificate), a RIF (retirement income fund), and a number of others. The bank would likely ask you to name a beneficiary on the account. This is done to prevent probate. However, remember the story about my father and learn from it. If there is only one person that you want to give your money to, then that is fine, but if there are multiple people, you must name them all.

PROTECT YOURSELF

In order to open this discussion, we need to go back to the reason everyone comes to Canada in the first place. We all know the answer to that one: to build a better life for your family. At the same time, we need to recall your greatest asset. It's you, and if you go down, everything that you worked for could be lost. So we are going to address a very important issue, income replacement. This is generally broken down into two areas; disability coverage and critical illness coverage.

Disability coverage: Disability insurance is meant to replace part of your income (usually 55%) in case of injury or illness. Now, the first thing to know is that not all disability policies are equal. Some give you the right see your own doctor—some do not. And that makes all the difference. The first group of claimants tends to be entrepreneurs who don't want to be away from their jobs any longer than the insurance company wants them to be. The second group of claimants tends to be more the corporate type, a type that encompasses malingerers—those people who are in no rush to get back to work after an injury or illness—the type that breeds distrust in the insurance companies. Make sure you're in the first group.

Integration of benefits: What this means is that if you signed up for a $2,000/month disability policy and you get hurt, and another organization also agrees to pay you let's say $1,200/month, whether it is another insurance company, Workers Safety Insurance Board, the employer, or whomever, then your insurance company only has to pay you the difference of $800/month. You can find policies that don't have this clause.

Return of Premium: What if you are lucky and never get injured? How would you like to get all your money back when you retire, tax free? Yes, there are disability policies available that have this benefit.

Soft tissue injuries/back injuries/sprains/strains: This is another very important feature. Many disability providers are so concerned about people faking injuries that they won't pay out unless something shows up on an X-ray. You don't want a policy like that. You want a policy that will cover you in all cases of injury or illness.

Injury occurs on or off the job: Many employers who provide a benefit plan to their employees will have disability coverage that only covers on the job accidents. While better than nothing, statistically, the average Canadian is more likely to get hurt in a car accident, at home, or while participating in sports and leisure than actually getting hurt on the job. That' the kind of coverage you want.

No limit on number of claims made: This one is fairly self-explanatory.

Make sure your provider does not have a clause where they can terminate your coverage if you make too many claims.

Critical Illness/Hospital Sickness Benefits: Let's imagine that you or your spouse were diagnosed with a terminal illness or a debilitating disease. The ill person might wish to do their "bucket list," go back to visit the homeland, see the Seven Wonders of the World, or take a cruise around the world. But from where would the money come? Cash in RRSPs? Sell the house? Remortgage the house? The problem with doing that is it ruins the whole game plan of coming to Canada to build a better life for your children and your children's children.

This is the reason that critical illness coverage exists in a place that already has state funded health care.

And just like disability coverage, it is possible to get critical illness coverage with a Return of Premium Clause, meaning that if you remain in good health, you get your money back at the end.

LIFE INSURANCE

There are many different types of life insurance. It is vitally important for you to know the differences so that you can pick the type that is the right one for your situation.

Reason for life insurance: Do you have massive debt from a mortgage or business loan that if all goes well you will have paid off before retirement? Or do you want to leave your family a lump sum of money for a particular purpose, regardless of whether you die young or old? These two situations require (differing) insurance products.

The standard formula that the insurance industry uses for determining the amount of coverage is: ten times annual salary plus debt. So if you make the average Canadian income of about $50,000 per year and have a three hundred thousand dollar mortgage, then the calculation would be to have $800,000 in coverage.

Term Insurance: Term insurance would be better understood by the public if it were renamed "temporary insurance." With term insurance you are buying a window of time. If you die in that window of time, the insurance company writes a cheque to your beneficiary. If you die outside that window, they cut no cheque at all.

Permanent insurance: Permanent insurance is frequently known by its official name, whole life insurance. If the reason for buying is that you need some security to pay off your debts if you die young, then term is the way to go, but if you want to leave a lump sum to your family whether you die next year or in sixty years, then you will want a permanent product.

Term to 100: Term to 100 is a rather unique type of life insurance that is sort of a hybrid between term insurance and permanent insurance. As we have already read, the disadvantage of a term policy is that it eventually runs out, but the advantage is lower premiums. The disadvantage of whole life coverage is that the premiums are high, but the advantage is that it lasts forever. What if you could get a policy that never runs out but that has the lower premiums more associated with term insurance? Great, right? That's why many companies don't offer the product. But you can find it, if that is what you want.

No Medical Insurance: No medical insurance is frequently called other names such as final expense insurance, funeral insurance, burial insurance, guaranteed issue insurance, instant issue insurance, and perhaps a few other names. It is frequently advertised by way of television commercials, and mail flyers delivered by the post office. The target client is often a retiree whose term insurance has now expired but who still wants to leave a lump sum when he or she dies. People with health problems who will never qualify for standard application coverage also tend to buy this type of policy.

Universal Life: This is another type of whole life policy. It can be a bit complicated, so I'm going to give a brief explanation of this product here. With a universal life policy, a portion of your premium goes into an investment. Over the years, the idea is for the investment to grow substantially. A universal life policy with a face amount of $100,000 would have an additional investment portion attached to it, so after a few decades the policy might pay out in total $150,000, $200,000 or more. Although this seems like a great idea, low interest rates over the past several years have made many people who hold a universal life policy realize that the projected payout at the end is going to be considerably lower than what the agent had suggested way back when the policy was first taken out.

The moral of this story is to make sure you sit down with a financial professional who will do a "needs analysis."

PLANNING FOR RETIREMENT

RRSP stands for Registered Retirement Savings Plan. An RRSP isn't an investment, it's a shell in which you can store all sorts of different kinds of financial plans and investments.

An RRSP could contain stocks, bonds, mutual funds, segregated funds, Guaranteed Investment Certificates, syndicate mortgages, Guaranteed Investment Accounts, just to name some of the more popular products that a typical Canadian RRSP might contain.

What an RRSP does is let you defer income tax. It is designed for Canadians who know that they are going to be bringing in less money after they retire than they are currently bringing in now. Canada Revenue Agency (CRA) charges income tax on a sliding scale depending on the income of the person. Someone who doesn't earn much income may pay no income tax at all, where someone with a high income might pay out 40% of their pay to income tax.

Life Income Fund: A life income fund generally comes from a company pension. Some employers offer a company matched retirement plan, meaning that whatever you put into it, they will contribute an equal amount. When you leave the company, it is recommended that you do something with it. The reason is that if the company runs into financial trouble, your retirement fund could be gone, or at least reduced. It has happened before, and will most likely happen again. Instead, if you quit, get downsized, or retire, you should move that money out of there and put it with an investment firm. That way, the success of your former employer will have no influence on the fund.

Various investments

Mutual funds are what are known as securities. The agent or broker must hold a license regulated by each provinces securities commission. Mutual funds are really just a collection of various stocks. They were designed for the purpose of the small investor being able to get into the stock market without a large cash outlay and with a lower risk. There are thousands of different funds out there, and virtually all of them are quite heavily diversified. This is both good news and bad news. The good news is that if one or a few of the companies that are inside that particular mutual fund take a huge nose dive, it won't cause your fund to drop too dramatically. The bad news is really the opposite side of the same coin. If a few of the stocks in the fund soar tremendously, your fund won't go up all that much because of all the other stocks in there that remain steadfast or have dropped. Mutual funds have no guarantees whatsoever, so if your fund dropped way down, you have only two choices: you can cash out at a loss, or you can hold onto it for enough years and hope that it rebounds satisfactorily. Mutual funds are also subject to fees known as Management Expense Ratios, or MER. If your fund's MER is 2%, then on a one hundred thousand dollar investment, expect to pay two thousand dollars per year in fees.

Segregated funds are very similar in concept to mutual funds. Segregated funds are sold by life insurance companies. Many financial experts describe segregated funds as "mutual funds with an insurance policy wrapper". Segregated funds must be kept separate from the insurance company's regular finances, hence the name. A "seg" fund and a mutual fund may both be investing in the same stocks, the main difference between the two, is there is a guarantee with a seg fund. The guarantee in a seg fund is generally either 75% or 100% of the original investment, depending on which plan you take. That means that you are guaranteed to get back either 75% or 100% of your money, even if the fund loses money. You will have to hold onto the fund for an agreed upon length of time, usually ten years to get this guarantee. And it is important to know that this guarantee is not free. A seg fund will have extra fees associated with it to cover this guarantee. If you cash out before the agreed upon time, you get what is in the fund, whether it has gained money or lost money, less any fees. If the seg fund rises in value, most plans will allow you to "reset" the guaranteed amount to this higher amount, however, that would mean that doing this will reset the amount of time, usually ten years, that you must hold the fund.

Depending on which plan you take, 75% or 100%, if you die while the funds are down, your beneficiary will receive 75% or 100% of the fund.

Guaranteed Investment Certificate (GIC): A GIC is a savings account where the interest rate is pre-set. There is an amount of time, generally two years, three years, four years, or five years that you must keep the money in the account in order to obtain that interest rate. If you withdraw the funds earlier than that date, you won't get the agreed upon interest rate. The longer you keep the money locked up, the higher the interest rate you can get.

Guaranteed Investment Account (GIA): The simplest way to describe a GIA is that it is like a GIC, except it is carried by insurance companies, just like seg funds, and the guarantee activates in the event of the contract holder's death.

If the contract holder dies while having a GIA, the company guarantees the highest of the two following things: either the balance of the account on the date of death; or 100% of the sum invested in this account.

Syndicated Mortgages: A developer who wants to build a condo tower, a commercial office building, or any other large construction project can generally only get conventional bank financing up to a certain percentage of the cost of the project. The remainder of the amount he needs has to come from someplace else. When you agree to give the developer your money, you go on title, the same way that your bank is on title for your house, if you have a mortgage. Syndicated mortgages have been around for a long time, but ordinary folk like you and me have only started hearing about them in the past few years. The reason is that they used to be reserved for those with very large sums to invest, like a million dollars. It was only relatively recently that the industry opened up the market dramatically by lowering the minimum investment to twenty five thousand dollars. Generally, the syndicate mortgages that have come across my desk pay 8% per annum, simple interest. It is important to know the difference between simple interest and compound interest. With compound interest, you receive interest on your interest, but with simple interest you do not. A typical syndicate mortgage locks your money away for a period of time, frequently three or four years.

Gold and other precious metals: The only reason that I am even mentioning this topic is because I am told that there are people on the radio urging us to buy gold. On the financial security pyramid or pillars, or ladder, or however you would like to refer to it, precious metals are to be considered at the top, right up there with collecting works of art. This means that it is something that would be recommended to do after your house is mortgage free, and you have amassed considerable wealth and assets.

REAL ESTATE

Buy vs Rent: There are always those who debate whether or not it is better to rent and invest more in the market, or buy real estate, and subsequently have less money left over at the end of the month to invest. Remember that home ownership has two entirely separate goals. The first one is to make money on it, either by buying low and selling high, or by making improvements to the property, thus increasing its value, or by paying off the mortgage so that you no longer have the expense of making payments. The second goal is to improve your quality of life. You have your very own residence without being at the mercy of a landlord, should they decide to sell the property, or raise the rent, or move into it themselves, or move a relative into it. You also have total control over what colour you would like the walls painted, the types of light fixtures, window coverings, faucets, countertops, and a host of other features.

Buying Real Estate: The first thing you will require is the **minimum down payment**. When you buy with less than twenty percent down, this is what the banks refer to as a high ratio mortgage. This requires you to have mortgage default insurance. The most popular organization the banks use to obtain mortgage default insurance is the Canada Mortgage and Housing Corporation (CMHC), a crown corporation. Two other companies that offer this are Genworth Financial Canada, and Canada Guaranty. They will charge a fee, and blend it into your payment. This can only be avoided by having a minimum of twenty percent of the purchase price of the property already saved up and available. For a first time home buyer, this could be difficult. Most of the property purchases I have made had CMHC on them. I still found this to be the lesser of the evils when compared to paying rent.

Next, you will need to **obtain approval for the mortgage**. You should do this before looking at any properties. There are two ways of doing this. The first is to talk to your own bank branch. The second is to use a mortgage broker. The advantage of using a mortgage broker is twofold. First, they do all the work, don't charge you and get paid a referral fee from the financial institution where the mortgage is placed. The second advantage is that they will frequently work with multiple lenders, giving them and you more choices. One thing they will be looking for is your Total Debt Service Ratio (TDSR). This means that all your payments, mortgage, utilities, and other things such as car loan payments and line of credit payments should not exceed approximately forty percent of your overall gross household income. So first of all, you should not be considering real estate if you owe any money on anything else, and yes, that includes your car.

The next thing is your need to have established a **credit rating**. There are two credit rating services. The most popular one is Equifax, and the other one is TransUnion. You can obtain your credit score from these institutions yourself at no charge. They will probably try to get you to pay for it, and they will quite likely offer you the information instantly if you pay, but you can wait and get it the slow way without having to pay. If you are new to the country, or young, or both, you may not have established a credit rating. The first thing is to have a credit card. Obviously, the intended goal is to pay the balance off every statement, thus avoiding any interest payments. If you think you can get by in this world without a credit card, you thought wrong. Not only is it vital in establishing a credit rating, but without one, it is generally quite difficult to purchase anything online, obtain tickets for a major event, rent a car, book a flight, stay in a hotel, and a host of various other situations that will cross your path from time to time.

Types of properties: There are really only four: condo, townhouse, semi, and detached

Condo is short for condominium. You will usually see them in the form of high rise buildings, but there are townhouse condos and even detached condos. With a condo you only own the inside, the condo corporation owns the outside. I'm using simple terminology here. You pay a monthly fee to them and they are responsible for exterior things like the roof, landscaping, snow removal, elevators, and really everything this is not inside your unit.

The next type of property on the scale is the **townhouse**. They can be condos or freehold. If it is a townhouse condo, you pay a fee to the condo corporation, just like a high rise, and they look after the same things like the roof, snow removal, and grass cutting. If it is a freehold, you own the whole thing, and you are responsible for everything. The main items to think about with a townhouse is that you share your walls with someone else.

Next on the list is the **semi-detached**. This has all the same possible downsides as a townhouse, but you are only sharing one wall. The key to a good semi is to have a great neighbour on the other side of the wall. But of course, you have very little way of finding that out until you are already moved in.

A **detached house**, meaning that it is not connected to any other building (you can walk all the way around all four sides), is the ultimate goal, in my humble opinion. In many regions, especially in the Greater Toronto Area (GTA), the detached house is sought after not only for the buffer zone between neighbours, but because many of these houses are ideally suited to having a separate basement apartment with a separate entrance, frequently a side door. This is an excellent way to bring in extra money to offset the high mortgage payment.

GOVERNMENT RETIREMENT BENEFITS

There are five main areas about which you will need to know: Canada Pension Plan (CPP), Canada Pension Plan Survivor Benefit, Canada Pension Plan Death Benefit, Old Age Security (OAS) and Guaranteed Income Supplement (GIS).

The Canada Pension Plan (CPP) is something that you would have paid into during the course of your working career. You can apply for it as early as age sixty or as late as age seventy. If you apply for it at age sixty, you will, however, receive a 36% reduction in benefits. If you apply for it at age seventy, you will get an increase of 42%.

According to the government of Canada statistics as of the year 2015, the average CPP monthly benefit is $619 and the maximum is $1,065.

Old Age Security: The Old Age Security (OAS) is a benefit for which you can apply at age sixty five, as of now, however, there are plans to increase the age at which you can apply to age sixty seven. Time will tell if the federal government sticks to the plan of age sixty seven, or if successive governments decide to roll it back to age sixty five. At time of publishing, the OAS is around $565 per month, however, it is indexed to inflation, so it generally goes up a few dollars per month every year.

CPP Survivor Benefit: If you are the first to die in a spousal or common-law relationship, the surviving spouse should apply for this benefit. It is generally 60% of the deceased partner's monthly CPP benefit, or if death occurs before age sixty five, then this benefit is calculated on the amount that it would have been if death had occurred at age sixty five.

CPP Death Benefit: Only a very few countries offer this benefit. To be eligible for your estate to receive this benefit you must have made contributions to CPP in the lesser of: one third of the calendar years in your CPP contributory period, but no less than three calendar years; or ten calendar years.

The amount of the death benefit depends on how much and for how long the deceased contributed to the CPP. The maximum benefit is $2,500. According to the latest statistics, the average benefit is around $2,300. The CPP death benefit is calculated as the amount equal to six months' worth of your monthly CPP benefit.

Guaranteed Income Supplement (GIS): If you live in Canada and have a low income, this monthly non-taxable benefit can be added to your Old Age Security (OAS) pension, if your annual income (or in case of a couple, your combined income) is less than the maximum annual income. The Canadian government calculates this maximum annual income amount based on numerous different criteria such as if you are single, widowed, or divorced, or if you have a spouse that receives the full OAS pension, or if your spouse does not receive the OAS, or if your spouse is already receiving the GIS and the OAS. You can always go the government's website yourself when you need this information: www.servicecanada.gc.ca

FINAL ARRANGEMENTS

This section will be dealing with an area that most people are not particularly thrilled about discussing. Furthermore, most people are not willing to walk into a funeral home and ask questions. Fortunately, I worked in the industry for ten years, so I'm in the position to not only help you spare your family a lot of grief and hardship, but at the same time, save you money as well.

There are two ways to pre-arrange your funeral: One way is to pre-arrange but not pre-pay. The other, and more preferred way, is to pre-arrange and pre-pay.

Cremation verses Burial: The main reason that 90 % of the people I have talked to about funerals over the years choose cremation, is so they can avoid the cemetery completely.

If you choose cremation, there are five options open to you regarding the disposition of the remains.

1. Your family can take the urn home with them and put it on the shelf. (This is not for everyone, some like the idea, some hate it.)

2. You can have the ashes scattered. Note: this choice is completely legal.

3. If you have an immediate family member that is already in a cemetery plot, most cemetery boards will allow you to place your urn in your family member's plot, generally for a fee of a few hundred dollars.

4. You can purchase your very own plot and have your urn buried there.

5. Cemeteries have structures called columbariums, or wall niches, that you can purchase for the purpose of having your urn placed there permanently.

Funeral Service Choices: For the sake of simplicity, there are really only three.

1. **A Direct Disposition.** All this means is that you are hiring the services of a licensed funeral director to send a transfer vehicle to your place of death, whether that is a hospital, a nursing home, or your own home. They will pick up the remains and transport them back to the preparation room at the funeral home, arrange for the cremation and return the ashes to you.

2. **A Memorial Service** contains everything a direct disposition contains, but the funeral establishment puts on a service, either in their own building, or in the church of your choice. Sometimes people want it to be held in a different location, such as a club that has their own facilities. It is important to note that with a memorial service, the body is not present, no casket is present, cremation has already taken place, and most often, the urn is present in lieu of a casket.

3. **A Traditional Service**: This is the type of arrangement where the casket is present. I'm not sure why, but many people are under the misconception that a traditional service is not available with cremation. The facts are that there are only two real differences between a traditional service with cremation to follow, and a traditional service with burial to follow. The first difference is that with burial, there is a funeral procession from the funeral home or church to the cemetery, and with cremation to follow, there is not, because the body has to be transported to the crematorium. The second difference is that with burial, a casket is purchased, and the casket is buried. But with cremation, the funeral home usually provides the use of the casket for the visitation and service, and hidden inside the casket underneath the white satin lining, where

no one can see, is the combustible, rigid, leak-proof container that is always necessary with cremation.

"I'm donating my body to science!"

This is what you need to know with regards to whole body donation. Medical schools, or schools of anatomy will accept body donations to train future medical professionals. It is completely different than donating organs. The body must be in very good condition and there must be a need for the body. It is important to remember that if you have a pre-paid funeral and you are accepted by a medical school, the pre-paid funeral fund will be returned to the family with interest.

SUMMARY

What do all of these things I've been talking about have in common? The greatest point of all that I've written here is that there are many ways for you to achieve wealth and grow it. An early mortgage and long-term investments can result in a free home for your loved ones to live in, money for them to live on and funds to grow even more money. They can even take the money they used to pay rent with and purchase yet more investments, so that when the third generation matures, there is a literal fortune waiting for them to inherit.

We also discussed investment vehicles such as real estate, mutual funds and term deposits, touching on various types of each, the idea being to make you aware of the choices you have moving forward. We even talked about how to protect your earning potential with disability insurance and life insurance. The chapter ended with a looked at funeral planning.

You came to Canada to make a better life for your family. This chapter can set you on the proper path to achieve what you wish. Good luck in all you do!

One Step at a Time

Parents, Educators and Children with Autism share their success stories

Anne-Carol Sharples

We all have aspirations and dreams for our children. Sometimes these expectations begin during our own childhoods as we dream about becoming parents. Sometimes the hopes and dreams do not begin until we look into the eyes of our newborn. No matter when the dream begins, no one dreams of autism. The diagnosis is a sucker-punch that leaves parents reeling and confused. Life quickly becomes complicated with all kinds of well-meant advice from professionals, family and strangers which include everything from medication to diet to the latest new therapy. This chapter does not offer advice on medicines, diet or therapies. The intention of this chapter is to uplift and inspire you. Perhaps you lay awake at night wondering, how I can fight the stigma related to the diagnosis. Maybe you cry, not because of who your child is, but because your child will not fit into the mold society expects. Please sit back and take a moment to learn about the successes of these autistic children and adults. It is with much love and respect that this chapter is dedicated to people on the autism spectrum as well as their families, teachers and caregivers.

SASHA

Sasha met all of her developmental milestones up until 22 months of age. It was then that the gregarious toddler fell silent. The daughter who was stringing two words together saying "What's this?" with inquisitive eyes vanished. Games and activities that Sasha once enjoyed no longer interested her. Eye contact became fleeting and she rarely responded to her name anymore. Sensing red flags, Sasha's parents Marjorie and Ryan began piecing the puzzle together. Shortly after, Sasha was diagnosed with autism. Devastated, but determined to bring back the vivacious child they once knew, the family began a courageous journey that would challenge every aspect of their personal relationships.

Investigating therapies, spending what seemed like hours on the phone and placing Sasha on waitlists left them disconcerted and worn out. Turning to one another for support, they drew upon each other's strengths and continued to map out the next steps in the journey. Together they discussed therapy options, and often reached for the other's hand when either one awoke panic stricken in the middle of the night, worried if they were doing the right thing.

Engaging Sasha in experiences and pulling her out of her shell that she so often retreated into became their undertaking. Sasha began Intensive Behavioral Intervention Therapy (IBI) on a daily basis. Family outings and activities took place every weekend. Rather than shielding Sasha from the world that overwhelmed her, her family wanted her to experience it in positive ways.

Sasha continued IBI until she turned four. It was then that Marjorie and Ryan registered her at the neighborhood school. Beginning kindergarten proved to be very challenging for Sasha and her family. The one-to-one therapy she'd been receiving each weekday was a stark contrast to the room filled with twenty-five boisterous children. IBI Therapy was usually quiet and controlled; the kindergarten classroom was anything but quiet! Sasha was overwhelmed and the first few weeks of school were traumatic for her. As Sasha entered the classroom each day a change would come over her. Her muscles tensed, arms and legs flailed, hands became fists and her jaw clamped shut. Sasha was in protective, fight mode. She was uncommunicative, confused and often distressed, making it impossible to participate in classroom activities. When the other children would sit in circle time and share their stories, she'd become increasingly agitated. Sasha's parents were quite concerned as she collapsed with exhaustion at the dinner table each evening, but they knew her adjustment would take time and vowed to continue taking her to school. What they did not know then, was that school would be the turning point for their daughter.

Marjorie and Ryan decided to use their beloved family outings as a way for Sasha to engage at school. They began to send in pictures of her with short anecdotes written on them. There were pictures of Sasha with her pet bird, at the pumpkin patch, visiting the zoo and opening presents on her birthday. On each of these pictures, Marjorie wrote about each day and what was occurring in the photograph. Over time, Sasha began to respond to these photos when her teacher shared them with her classmates during circle time. Slowly, with support from her teacher, Sasha began to sit for circle time. She'd become very excited when she saw a picture of herself. Sasha's teacher, Mrs. Watson, knew she wanted to share the stories of the pictures herself, so she would have Sasha stand beside her and share her stories through pointing and babbling. Sasha was beginning to communicate at school.

Mrs. Watson played a vital role in Sasha's success at school; for instance, she recognized that Sasha was overwhelmed by the large number of students in the class, so she assigned her a spot right next to her during circle time. She also introduced a visual schedule so that Sasha would know what to expect throughout her day. When there was an unanticipated disruption in her schedule, Mrs. Watson used an "Oops" card to demonstrate the change. Sasha began to communicate with Mrs. Watson by babbling and pointing to the pictures on her schedule. When she was hungry, she pointed to a picture of "snack." She even began to switch her schedule around to her preferred activities and would giggle while proudly showing Mrs. Watson the changes she had made. Sasha grew to love Mrs. Watson; she had a gentle tone of voice and made everyone feel welcome in her classroom. She made school fun for all of her students and her love for teaching shone through her interactions with the students. In addition to utilizing the photographs Sasha's parents sent in, she also recognized Sasha's love for books. Mrs. Watson provided her with a copy of the story she was reading to the class each day. Sasha could hold her book and look at the pictures while Mrs. Watson read aloud to the class. This was a simple yet effective way of keeping her engaged during story time.

Sasha was fortunate to have Mrs. Watson as her Senior Kindergarten teacher the following year. This is the year she began to speak. It began with a word mixed in with gibberish and pointing. It was easy enough to understand, so whoever Sasha was communicating with could model the appropriate language. Soon she began stringing two words together, then two became four so that "blah, blah backpack" became, "I want my backpack."

Sasha is now in first grade and loves school; she reads, writes and talks constantly. The other students adore Sasha because she is persistent, passionate and a joy to be around. She loves to share stories of family outings with her teachers and classmates, with or without photographs.

HENRY

When our son, Henry, was three years old, we were told that he'd never speak or be able to perform simple tasks. We watched, on pins and needles, as the developmental evaluator modeled the activity of stacking three blocks on top of each other and held our breath as she handed the blocks to Henry for him to duplicate what she'd done. Our hearts broke when he was unable to even attempt to stack them. After this evaluation, his father and I were told that Henry would need to be institutionalized. After the shedding of countless tears and multiple late night discussions, we knew that we would not put our son in an institution. We refused to give up hope that we could find a way to help Henry. We enrolled Henry in a school that offered special needs classrooms.

We were fortunate to find a wonderful group of teachers who worked tirelessly to see that Henry was able to function to the best of his ability. After two years in school, with the inclusion of daily therapy, he was able to communicate, albeit in a limited way. Henry never entered a mainstream classroom, but he has achieved multiple successes. The educators and assistants in Henry's special needs classrooms refused to accept the idea of can't. They repudiated the limitations that had been placed on Henry by various doctors and educational evaluators. They only saw what Henry could do and the sky was the limit as far as they were concerned.

Over the years Henry learned how to not only stack blocks, but to tie his shoes and dress himself. He will never hold a job or live by himself, but Henry has made huge strides from what we were originally told he would be able to accomplish. We know that institutionalization would not have been the best choice for Henry as he never would have progressed to the level that he is at today.

ABIGAIL

Here it was again, the dreaded block test. Abigail's grandmother, Eleanor, rolled her eyes as she watched the evaluator hand the blocks to Abigail. She knew Abigail would not stack the blocks or build the bridge the evaluator had shown her. Why are these blocks so important anyway she wondered? Abigail was four years old and had missed most of the developmental milestones. She was not yet speaking coherently; in fact, Abigail had little interest in speaking and seemed unconcerned if her needs were not met. She was absorbed by her own world and took little notice of anything occurring around her. Eleanor wondered if this was because Abigail's mother had abandoned her when she was eighteen months old. She suspected the troubles were compounded by issues in addition to abandonment and was not surprised by the diagnosis of autism. She was surprised when the healthcare professionals told her that Abigail would likely never speak or communicate because she was locked inside her own world. Institutionalization was mentioned, but quickly dismissed by Eleanor. She knew there was more for Abigail and held on to hope that she would find help for Abigail.

As it turned out, help was found during Abigail's first year of school. She started out at age five, a year behind most of the other children in the Junior Kindergarten class. Abigail's teachers and support staff read through the medical and behavioral evaluations and chose a course of action: Abigail was taught just as the other children were taught, with patience, love and repetition. Her teachers did not become frustrated when Abigail stared blankly and did not repeat the sounds they were asking her to make. Instead, they simply tried again the next day. Gradually, Abigail began to come out of her shell, appearing more aware and less self-absorbed. She haltingly began to repeat sounds, then words.

After two years of kindergarten, Abigail was speaking and able to communicate her needs and desires. Her comprehension moved more slowly; it was not until grade three that Abigail began to understand that she should take off her jacket when she felt warm. Her schoolwork moved slowly, as well. Her teachers spent extra time working with her each day and she worked with her grandmother and tutors in the afternoons and throughout summers.

Over the years, Abigail spent countless hours working after school with her tutors and teachers. Her grandmother worked tirelessly to see that Abigail reached her goals. Abigail graduated from high school and is now living on her own in an apartment with two other girls. She even has her dream job working at an amusement park she loved going to as a child.

MARIAH

My name is Mariah and I am twenty-one years old and I have autism. What autism means for me is that I am an excellent painter. I paint better than your average person does. I used to go to school, but now I am finished with school and can paint any time I want. This is very exciting for me because I love to paint; it's my favorite thing to do! My dad takes me and my paintings to art shows where we sell the paintings. My dad always says to do what you love and you will be happy.

MARIAH'S DAD

Mariah struggled with school. She is an excellent reader, but struggles with short-term memory and cannot recall recently taught basic math functions. She was teased often and never understood why the other kids didn't behave as she thought they should. She would often tell the other children what to do, an action that did not win her many friends. She didn't understand the rules of the playground and would push other kids off the swings when she wanted a turn. Her mother and I worried that she'd never be able to hold a job due to her lack of social skills and memory struggles. We wanted more for Mariah. We can provide for her financially, but wanted her life to have quality. We wanted Mariah to be joyful and content.

When she was in her first year of high school, Mariah took an art class and fell in love with painting. She loves the vivid colors and the feel of the paint. Her art teacher recognized that, not only did Mariah have a talent for painting, but that painting was restorative for Mariah. If Mariah was having a rough day at school, her teacher would bring her to the art room where she could calm herself with paint. Her mother and I were stunned at the artwork she brought home. Painting gives Mariah joy. She loves to go to art shows and speak with people about her paintings; she could talk about her paintings for hours! She has felt true success by giving enjoyment to others with her artwork. Since she is able to experience other people's reactions to her paintings, she is inspired to continue working on her craft. Mariah's struggles with interacting with other people evaporate when she speaks of her art. People may not understand Mariah's way of thinking, but they understand her art.

Art is the desire of a man to express himself, to record the reactions of his personality to the world he lives in. Amy Lowell, poet

LILY AND CHARLENE

Charlene will never forget the first day she met Lily. At that time, Lily's only way of communicating was to scream. Lily was four years old, an only child who lived in a low-income apartment with her father. At the time Charlene met her, Lily had received no prior intervention; she was a cautious girl who clung to her father's leg on that day in her apartment. While Lily's father was giving Charlene a snapshot of what the first four years of Lily's life had been like, Lily let it be known that she was displeased with the disruption to her routine. She screamed, climbed the furniture, and removed her clothing in protest. The volume of her screams pierced the air and her father worried that the neighbors would complain, yet again, about the noise. Her father explained that he had been unable to accomplish basics, such as getting Lily to sit in a chair to eat.

The years of struggle, both financial and emotional, wore on his face; he was desperate for help. His spirit was broken, beaten down by the everyday demands of life and compounded by his daughter's needs and his inability to understand her. Charlene desperately wanted to help and felt as though she were carrying a load of bricks as she walked away from their apartment, weighted down by the father's anguish for his daughter.

Charlene went to the school where she was employed as a support worker to speak with the principal about helping Lily. Principal Anderson's son is on the autism spectrum, so he related to the anguish Lily's father was experiencing. Plans were made and Lily began Junior Kindergarten the following week. To say that Lily's first day was exhausting for not only Lily, but also her dad and the staff would be an understatement. The five minute walk from their apartment building to the school took more than half an hour as Lily battled her father every step of the way. Upon arrival at school, it took another fifteen or so minutes for Lily's dad to convince her to enter the building. She made it to the threshold of the classroom and remained there all day long, screaming whenever anyone entered her space or tried to engage her. This continued for several weeks, and throughout that time Charlene persevered by remaining calm and respecting Lily's need for space. By doing this, Charlene gained Lily's trust along with the admiration of the classroom teacher and the staff within the school.

Charlene had a unique way of interacting with Lily; she understood that Lily's behavior was her only way of communicating. She treated Lily with dignity and respect and accepted her where she was. Charlene recognized how difficult school was for Lily and took baby-steps with her, acting as a guide who would remain with Lily until she was ready to go it alone. Over the weeks Lily moved from the threshold of the classroom door to learning how to sit inside the classroom, with Charlene at her side. This was accomplished with patience and kindness, but also with a song. "Row, Row, Row Your Boat" was sung to alert Lily that it was time to enter the classroom and sit down. Lily liked the song and began to request it by holding her hands out and rocking back and forth. Charlene found an old wooden boat and brought it into the classroom so that Lily could sit in the boat and rock it from side to side. This was a motivating experience for Lily since she loved to rock. It is from sitting in the boat that Lily learned how to sit in a chair.

Charlene shared the idea of singing the song with Lily's father. He began singing the song at home to alert Lily that it was time to sit down to eat. Her father was overjoyed when Lily joined him at the table, sat in a chair and shared a meal with him. Charlene was able to accomplish so much with Lily by taking the time to get to know and understand her. It is individuals like Charlene, who have an innate ability to be present and want to help, that make peoples' hearts smile. Lily's father's heart was smiling by the end of her Junior Kindergarten year as he found hope for his daughter's future.

CAITLIN

Mondays are the best. At least Caitlin thinks so because Monday is horseback riding day. Caitlin is fifteen years old and has been diagnosed with autism, in addition to several other health concerns. Caitlin does not have much energy and, as a general rule, does not enjoy exercise. However, she loves all things horse-related; she enthusiastically shows up for her horseback riding lesson and will brush her horse and clean out his stall with gusto. Not every day goes so well. Caitlin struggles when things do not go as she expects and some days Caitlin becomes irritated with her horse and kicks or even punches him out of frustration. Caitlin is working on developing patience, accommodating changes to routine and communicating with her horse without kicking or punching.

Her mother is thrilled with the life lessons, as well as the Hippotherapy Caitlin has received and has shared Caitlin's successes with her special needs classroom teacher, Mrs. McFray. Being quite perceptive, Mrs. McFray decided to explore Caitlin's interest in other animals. She learned that Caitlin has a passion for all animals; therefore, Mrs. McFray incorporated a classroom unit on animals and even obtained a grant to purchase several animals for her classroom. The animals, which include a turtle, a bunny, two guinea pigs and a hedgehog have been a huge hit with all of the students in the special needs classroom.

Caitlin's favorite is the bunny, Mr. Cuddles. She loves to feed him mint and watch him motor his way through the stalk. The students have learned that they cannot hold or pet an animal when they are angry because the animal will become frightened. Prickles, the hedgehog, rolls into a tight ball when she is scared or hears loud noises. Mrs. McFray believes that her students know exactly how Prickles feels. The students can only hold Prickles when they are quiet and calm; they are learning to self-regulate in order to interact with a classroom animal. The classroom pets are treasured by all; therefore the students are highly motivated to regulate their emotions. Because Mrs. McFray took the time to listen to Caitlin's mom, ponder what she heard, and explore options for incorporating animals in her classroom, all of the students have benefited. Mrs. McFray has a deep affection for her students and wants to offer each of them the best learning environment possible.

MILES

Hi, my name is Miles and I'm fourteen years old. I always knew there was something different about me, and it was confirmed when I was seven and told that I have Asperger's Syndrome. Fitting in at school, or anywhere else, has always been difficult for me. I wanted friends, but couldn't figure out how to make them. Things would start out okay, but after a while I noticed that my friends would not be around our usual hangouts. Even worse, when they'd see me they would turn their backs or walk away. I never understood what I'd done wrong. Having friends, then immediately losing them was the hardest part of school for me. The schoolwork was easy-peasy and I probably could've done it with my eyes closed. Recess was a nightmare. At least it was a nightmare until I met Mrs. Wiley and began attending the Program to Assist Social Thinking, aka PAST. I dedicate this story to her. It is due to Mrs. Wiley that I am where I am today.

I began attending PAST one day a week when I was in third grade and I liked it from the start. The best part of PAST is that it is a safe place where we can be ourselves and not worry about anything. You see, all of the kids who attend PAST have autism. And, all of the teachers are super cool and completely understand us. I feel comfortable in my own skin and I can be me when I'm there. Now, that doesn't mean that everything is fun and easy. My teachers challenge me all the time. They know exactly how far to push me and understand when I become frustrated. In fact, they taught me how to control my emotions. Mrs. Wiley, my parents, and my third grade teacher, Mrs. Smyth, would come up with goals I needed to work on at school and at home. So, one of the items my mom really wanted me to learn was how to ask her how her day was and to be genuinely interested in her response. One of the items my teacher wanted me to do was to greet her every morning. Each day I was rated on my performance and scores were tallied up weekly. Once I mastered these goals, other goals were set.

What makes PAST so much fun is that we do super-cool activities, like going rock climbing or to the aquarium that has sea life from around the world. Also, we have a Bearded Dragon in our class! In fact, Eragon, our Bearded Dragon, is such a popular guy, I don't think he is ever in his cage. He has a calming effect on all of us when we are upset. Another activity we do is sit on extremely cool bean bag chairs and do role plays. We also play games to learn about all sorts of barriers that prevent us from being social thinkers. One of my barriers is that I get stuck on what I want to do all of the time. At PAST we have to learn to work as a team and not just do what we want to do. We have a marble jar and each of us puts a marble in the jar when we are being social thinkers. Once the jar is full, we go on an outing; it could be eating at a neighborhood restaurant or checking out the largest indoor reptile zoo. We vote on it and decide. My teacher says we are working, but it feels more like fun than work!

I now realize that my friends used to avoid me as a result of me always wanting things my way. I wanted to be the boss of the whole shebang, from a game of soccer to only talking about what I wanted to talk about. Now I understand that it is important to let other people talk and to listen to them, even if I'm not all that interested. Mrs. Wiley and PAST have taught me how to interact with others and how to have a conversation. Now I know how to start and continue a conversation. PAST has taught me about the perspective of others. I used to think that everyone thought the same way I do. Well, I sure was surprised to find out this isn't so!

Anne Wiley retired from her role as a PAST Teacher in 2014 but continues to volunteer and contribute to the Autism Department at the TCDSB.

Declutter Your Mind for Success

Erin Muldoon Stetson

"My baggage", "your baggage", "his baggage" —phrases thrown around in casual conversation as much as an actual suitcase is thrown around by handlers at an airport. What does it mean when we talk about our "baggage?" After all, we're not actually referring to that matching set of luggage your mother bought you after college, are we? No, we are talking about the emotional and life experience "stuff" you pick up along the way; the stuff that weighs you down and makes the inside of your head hurt.

When we take a trip, our baggage literally gets heavier and messier with each souvenir we add. And, if you're like me, you can't wait to unpack and put the dirty laundry in the wash where it belongs. Similarly, in life every experience comes with emotional as well as physical stuff. Unfortunately, not all of it is as pleasurable as the mementos from vacation. Plus, when unpacking, most of us take a look at what comes out of the suitcase so we can put it where it belongs.

But, when it comes to emotional baggage, people tend to stuff it away without really looking at it. What they are doing is filling up the emotional equivalent of a classic, overstuffed closet; the one where, when you open the door, a thousand things come crashing down on your head. The one where you don't open the door except maybe a couple inches now and then to stuff more things into the dark, scary closet.

On an emotional level, that stuffing is doing you no good at all. In fact, all that clutter is not relegated to your subconscious mind. It affects all parts of your mind, as well as your body and spirit. It causes pain, disease and emotional issues. It can block you in countless ways—from achieving your potential, living authentically and manifesting abundance in your life.

Why is your mind so cluttered in the first place? It's because you've been "collecting" experiences, memories and feelings for a lifetime. Even in the womb, there may have been alarming and confusing experiences. If you had a difficult birth, or traumatic first few moments of life, the imprint of those experiences is still with you. To add insult to injury, as a baby, you may have often struggled to be understood or to have your needs met while your bumbling care givers tried to figure out if you were hungry, sleepy or needed a diaper change. How frustrating that must have been. Those early experiences went into your collection.

Think about the clutter you have collected. I suggest that, as you read this, you jot down the thoughts that pop into your head. No doubt you will start to think of your own personal clutter that is stuffed inside you somewhere. Your notes will help you when you decide to clear that clutter out. Remember, you need to look at all of it squarely before you can put it away for good.

The collection of emotional clutter goes on throughout your life. In the toddler years, you stumble and fall (literally), and struggle to communicate only to be utterly misunderstood. Then, as a teen, you stumble figuratively as you try to find your way, and still find communication difficult as your values change in relation to those of parents, teachers or even your peers.

Think about it:

- A humiliating experience in class when a teacher scolded you in front of everyone.
- Someone you had a crush on treated you with contempt.
- A vicious, behind-the-back bullying campaign waged by an alleged "friend."
- A time when you were unkind or ungrateful to someone who didn't deserve it.
- The day you walked out of a store with a pack of gum you didn't pay for.

Each of these experiences is jarring. Every single one of them can disrupt the energy system in your body and mind. It's no wonder you feel so overwhelmed with the clutter.

I vividly remember something that happened when I was 12 years old. I received a scathing note from one of my "best friends" who happened to live across the street. It was poetic in its poignancy. "Erin, you think you're hot shit on a silver platter, but really you're just cold diarrhea on a paper plate!" Wow. That hurt. It's funny now —I mean really funny — and I'm so impressed with the verbiage. But at the time, I cried big tears —the kind of tears that I thought might never stop gushing. I had to re-think my whole persona. Did I really think that I was "hot shit?" And was I actually "just cold diarrhea?" I collected the anger, the sadness and the insecurity of that moment and buried it all in my mind, heart and body.

For the record, I'm not saying that any of the experiences I'm mentioning were bad, or good, for that matter. Nor am I saying that my friend in the "hot shit" story was wrong for writing that note. What I am saying is that our experiences stay with us, in one form or another, and often create disruptions in our energy systems.

Have you been able to jot down a few notes about memories of your own that may have stayed with you and created disruptions in your own life? Job struggles, relationship or parenting challenges, heartache, loss, trauma—the little things and the big things that may be stuffed away, buried, doing some damage unbeknownst to you.

All of these things go into your collection. Don't judge them. Don't judge yourself. Simply write down a "title" for the memory. We'll address it later and possibly let go of it with ease. You won't lose the memory, but merely the negative charge that is connected to it.

Now that you have started to examine your impressive collection, you can understand how it has grown exponentially over your lifetime. You can imagine how your mind has gotten cluttered. It's no wonder so many people feel weighed down, bottled up, distracted and even confused at times.

It is possible to declutter your mind if you have the proper tools. There is a process you can use to fix the effects of that build-up.

Pat yourself on the back for beginning this journey. It's going to be fun!

TAPPING

Tapping is based on Emotional Freedom Techniques (EFT). It is a relatively new discovery that has provided thousands with relief from pain, disease and emotional issues. It can alleviate the most common matters (fear of public speaking) to the most extreme (chronic debilitating back pain), and a wide array of "stuff" in between. Basically, tapping is mind/body healing. It is a combination of ancient Chinese knowledge and modern psychology.

Tapping produces a relaxation response in your body and mind and creates an emotional contentment in the present moment. It is wonderfully simple and effective, and it is accomplished by stimulating well established energy meridian points on your body.

"How do you do that?"

You do that by tapping on particular points with your fingertips while focusing on the issue at hand.

"Really?" "It's not more complicated than that?"

Yes, really. And no, it's not more complicated than that. Plus, the process is easy to memorize, and portable—you can do it anywhere. You only need your hands and your mind.

It is my goal to make this real healing easy and accessible to you. For the entrepreneur feeling overwhelmed, or the person who has dreams of starting a business but is blocked by fear, these techniques can help create such fundamental shifts that walls tumble and doors open. The healing path of body, mind and spirit lies ahead.

So how does tapping differ, say, from other energy healing modalities such as acupuncture? By focusing on the mind-body connection, EFT tapping harnesses the power of the mind and combines it with the body's energy to propel healing to a level that could not otherwise be achieved. The techniques essentially bring a psychotherapeutic element to the energy meridians long familiar to alternative healers.

The power of thought and its effects on our well-being are no longer considered theoretical. The evidence is piling up. So let's declutter your mind so that your thoughts no longer sabotage you but can have the impact you want them to!

EFT TAPPING IN ACTION

Let's look at a particular, very real scenario that will be familiar to many. I like to call it the fear of public writing. Now, we could also address the fear of public speaking or something else but, given the fact that I overcame my fear of public writing to write this chapter, it seems an apropos example. Additionally, the fear of public writing can be a huge deal for an entrepreneur, especially when you are expected to publish a blog, post on Facebook and update your website on a regular basis.

EFT tapping has the unique ability to handle your fears and turn them into calm cool action. Whether you feel paralyzed at the thought of doing an activity like writing, or are shy about sharing what you've already written, EFT tapping can help put those fears in check.

For example, have you hesitated to write a book because of your anxiety about the fact that the dreaded written word can never be erased? It will be "out there" speaking for you, for all time. If you are like I was, that thought paralyzes you. But here I am, writing this. And enjoying it, I might add. How am I able to face my fears so courageously?

As I mentioned above, the answer is quite simple and incredibly revolutionary. I can't wait to share this fabulous secret with you. Tap along with me. You won't be sorry. Then we can high five on the other side of this silly fear that's holding you back from your greatness.

EFT IN A NUTSHELL

The body contains a network of energy points and energy channels — actual locations that can be accessed through tapping. In addition to the physical act of tapping on these specific points, EFT involves the use of words. The power of words, of language, to channel and manifest intention is hardly in question any more. So with EFT, you will use words first to acknowledge the details of the negative — the big pieces of junk cluttering your mind.

Looking at them and facing them is the first step to releasing the junk you've been shoving into your suitcase for so long. Finally, positive language is used to manifest what you want to bring into your life after you've released the unwanted clutter through tapping.

So, let's return to our hypothetical case of a person (maybe you) who is afraid to write. This fear is getting in the way of your business, your success and your ability to create abundance in your life. Below are the simple steps that I would walk you through if you were this hypothetical person. In no time, you would be writing and publishing.

STEP 1

Close your eyes and think about what is holding you back from writing and publishing that book or updating your blog. Once you have something specific in mind, give it a number on a scale of 0-10, ten being the most intense. If you have many things running through your mind, write them down and start with the one specific issue that has the highest intensity. Think of it as the biggest piece of junk in that closet—the one that might actually knock you out if it fell on your head. Give that piece of junk a "title"—you don't need to write down the whole sordid history or explanation of the issue, just its title. The number you assign to that issue is extremely important. It allows you to compare how you feel before and after tapping.

For example, you may be thinking: "What if my ex reads this and thinks, 'what the %&*# is she writing about? Why was I ever with that chick? What a weirdo!'" Or perhaps you are thinking, "No one who reads this will ever want to talk to me, meet me or hire me. I'll be ruined."

Your title for this piece of mental debris might be: Fear of Rejection. Maybe it earns a level of 8, 9 or even 10, depending on how paralyzing it is. (You insert whichever number makes sense for how you feel in the present moment.)

STEP 2

Tap continuously with your fingers on each of the following spots while repeating the corresponding phrases out loud. (If you think a diagram might be helpful, please visit http://taponit.com.)

Karate Chop Spot (this is the place on the side of your hand you would use if you were to use a karate chop to break a piece of wood): Tap continuously with four fingers on that spot while saying the following phrase three times aloud: "Even though I am afraid of being judged and rejected [insert here: by my ex or by future clients] for what I write, I'm still a really good person."

- **Eyebrow point** (this is the beginning of your eyebrow closest to your nose): Tap continuously with two fingers at that spot and repeat the following phrase: "I'm afraid that my [ex or future client] is going to judge me and my writing in a negative way."

- **Side of eye** (this is the bone bordering the outside corner of your eye): Tap continuously with two fingers on that spot and repeat the following phrase: "What if my [ex or future client] reads what I wrote and thinks I'm a terrible writer?"

- **Under the eye** (about 1/2 inch below the eye on the bone): Tap continuously with two fingers, saying: "I'm nervous to put myself out there. I will be laughed at."

- **Under the nose** (this is the philtrum: the small indentation between the bottom of your nose and the top of your upper lip): Tap continuously with two fingers on that spot while you say: "I'm afraid that someone [my ex or a judgmental future client] is going to read my writing if I put it out there."

- **Chin** (the spot inside the indentation midway between the bottom of your chin and your lower lip): Tap continuously with two fingers on that spot and say: "I'm not sure if I can handle the embarrassment of having my writing judged by [my ex, a future client] or anyone else for that matter."

- **Collarbone**: Tap continuously with four fingers along your collarbone towards your breast bone. Say these words: "I'm not ready to have my thoughts and ideas critiqued and ridiculed."

- **Under arm** (four inches below your armpit, on the side of your body): Tap continuously with four fingers: "I'm nervous that [my ex or a future client] will read what I'm writing and make fun of me."

- **Crown of head**: Tap continuously with all five fingers in a circular motion on the top of your head: "I'm afraid that [my ex or anyone] is going to read my writing and laugh at me."

- **Eyebrow point**: "I'm okay now."

- **Side of eye**: "I can relax now."

- **Under the eye**: "I am calm and relaxed."

- **Under the nose**: "My confidence is growing."

- **Chin**: "I am feeling more and more confident about my writing."

- **Collarbone**: "I am excited to write an awesome [book, article, blog]."

- **Under arm**: "I can't wait to write my [book, article, blog]."

- **Top of head**: "I'm ready to write and publish an amazing [book, article, blog]."

When you are done, take a deep breath and hold it. Then let it out in a slow, smooth exhalation.

STEP 3

After completing the tapping and repetitions, reassess the intensity of your feelings about the topic (in this case, public writing), using the scale you used originally, from 0 to 10, with ten being the strongest. Write down your response, the number and something about how you feel. Comment about whether there were any qualitative changes to the way you view or feel about the topic. If your number is still high, then repeat the process.

Be clear in acknowledging any change. For example, "After tapping, my fear of rejection and judgment regarding my writing from [my ex or future clients] is at about a level two, down significantly from my previous level of eight."

The three steps outlined above are how you use EFT to overcome your fear of public writing. You can use the same format to cope with other issues that are holding you back. The phrases that you use in your repetitions during tapping will vary according to what you are trying to release. Here are some examples:

- **Karate Chop Spot**: "Even though I'm afraid that my family will disown me because what I want to write about is too off the grid for them, I have confidence and love. I forgive them for their potential judgments." Repeat three times.

- **Karate Chop Spot**: "Even though I fear that my ideas will change one day, and what I write will be 'out there' forever, reminding me of how foolish I was, I deeply and completely love and accept myself."

- **Karate Chop Spot**: "Even though my writing isn't perfect, it's a work in progress that never seems to end. I am whole, and complete, and fabulous just as I am right now, and so is my writing."

- **Karate Chop Spot**: "Even though I feel as if I don't have time to write, I am willing to make changes in my life because I deeply and completely love and accept myself."

The intended and very real outcome of EFT tapping in this circumstance is increased self-confidence. Whether it is your writing or something else that is standing in your way, your confidence will grow exponentially the more you tap. You will laugh at your previous fears. To use our example of fearing the reaction of your ex, once you have utilized EFT tapping, you might assume that, should he read your writing, he'll wonder how he ever let someone like you get away!

Our fears about what might happen are often times more intense than any actual, potential outcome. Tapping creates equilibrium between that fear and what is real. It will allow you to gain a calm, cool perspective regarding the debris that was weighing you down by cluttering up your suitcase or your closet –in other words, your mind!

Decluttering your mind through EFT tapping applies to literally any aspect of your life. It can help you find fulfillment, success, and enjoyment in any arena: relationships, money, body image, health etc. Starting with identifying what is holding you back, seeing it for what it is and then releasing it, you ultimately replace it with something positive that will help you move forward.

The things that are holding you back are all that junk we talked about earlier: Fears or objections (the "I can't" mentality), obstacles — perceived or real (time, logistics) — and ultimately your "story" – the belief system that holds you where you are instead of helping you get to where you want to be.

The process that works for your mind can also be used to declutter your body. There is a holistic connection between and among mind, body and spirit, which means that detoxing one will help you connect with the others to live your best life.

In using EFT techniques for the spirit, you will address matters of perspective, outlook and attitude. The law of attraction is essentially at work every time you succumb to fear or, conversely, feel optimistic. When you fear an outcome and fixate on that fear, you are focusing on what is essentially a belief system based on fear. Your mind, as well as your actions, reflects that belief system and you will manifest the very things you are afraid of.

When you can tap on and release the fear, you can recreate a belief system based on positive emotions, optimism and confidence. You become that person and your every action reflects those new beliefs.

So what does this mean for you? It means that EFT tapping can bring you more comfort, love and enjoyment in life. It can help you rid yourself of the heavy baggage and clutter that get in the way of being your most successful self.

To learn more about the benefits of tapping, please visit http://taponit.com.

Outshine the Competition: Coming Out on Top in the Interview Process

Ossy Botha

"Sometimes one creates a dynamic impression by saying something, and sometimes one creates as significant an impression by remaining silent."

– The Dalai Lama

Interview Dynamics introduces a concept which helps Career & Job Seekers prepare, refine and polish the "how & what" in any interview situation; how to describe and what to say about their skills and experiences. - Ossy

There are no two ways about it. Job-hunting in today's harsh economic realities is tougher than ever before. If the prospect of job interviews sends shivers up and down your spine, you're not alone. Global expansion and outsourcing, technological innovation and a spate of economic crises have changed the employment landscape beyond recognition, and a job-seeker is stepping into an unknown that few have wandered into before. In short, nailing the interview is much more of a priority than ever before.

There are new rules when it comes to looking for a job, and it's no longer just about possessing the right resumé. Whether you are fresh out of college, changing careers or wanting a promotion in your current company or current field, you have to go through an interview, come across as a credible candidate, and then show you are the best fit for the job. You have to deliver a flawless performance while juggling the stresses of applying for several jobs at the same time. It's a tremendous burden to bear, and it's no surprise that many applicants cringe at the thought of readying themselves for an interview. There are loads of how-to books on the shelves in bookstores and libraries, many of them filled with theory, tips and advice -- none of which you'll remember in the heat of an interview.

So, how do you really get up to speed to out-prepare and outshine the competition? The solution is quite simple. We help you gain the confidence and the assuredness you need so that, rather than stepping into the interview with clammy palms and nervous tics, you'll breeze in with a confident stride, a smile on your face and a strong handshake, and come out a winner.

WHAT IS INTERVIEW DYNAMICS AND ITS PURPOSE?

Each one of us performs various roles in our lives. You are a brother, son, boyfriend, colleague, uncle, husband or a mother, daughter, BFF, stepsister, aunt and so on. You take on the roles that are expected of you without question and switch from being parent to sibling in the blink of an eye.

Similarly, as a work colleague we take on our different profiles while we perform the various roles applicable to our job criteria, whether we are the Office Cleaner or the CEO.

In the office, you are a colleague and, simultaneously, a department head. You have to report to a board of several bosses and, at the same time, have to take care of several junior employees. You have to motivate the ranks below you, you have to sell new ideas to your bosses and you have to take care of all the paperwork! Basically, you wear several hats at work and, during the course of a workday, you move seamlessly from one role to another.

In Interview Dynamics, we help you to do the same. We teach you to think of yourself as a business, and we remove the personal ego from the preparation. The brutal truth is that, no matter how qualified you may be, there is always the possibility of someone more highly skilled than yourself. You can bone up as much as you can by reading books on interviewing, rehearsing your answers and doing your homework, but it's how you fare during your interview that seals your fate.

So, rather than have you present yourself as a nervous candidate, we take you step-by-step through the practicalities of preparing for an interview. We guide you through several processes and we help you change your mindset. There are many books on interviewing skills and they advocate that you brush up on your strengths and weaknesses, but do they tell you how to do just that?

When I was coaching a client through Interview Dynamics, I asked her to tell me about a mistake she had made at work. She was totally flabbergasted by the question and several awkward minutes ticked by and she still couldn't come up with an answer. Luckily, this was a practice run, and she subsequently used the tools in Interview Dynamics to prepare herself for the real thing.

We build your confidence through shifting your perspective in order to tap the infinite resources that already reside within you and to leverage the skills inherent in you to suit the occasion. The simple truth is that you are a multi-talented person and, rather than presenting yourself as a one-dimensional candidate to the employer, how about viewing yourself as a business which we call Firm You (Pty) Ltd?

This company, Firm You, has a range of services and products, namely your work experience, credentials and other qualities such as leadership, communication and motivational skills that will greatly benefit the end-consumer of the company you are interviewing with. In return for supplying these "goods and services", you are paid money, as you would in any business transaction, in the form of a salary.

Residing within you, waiting to be called to the fore, are several important figures of authority in the business – the Managing Director, the Financial Director, the Sales Director and the Project Director. Depending on the task at hand during the interview, you will wear the hat that most suits the role you are playing. For example, during that phase of interview when you have to persuade the (slightly skeptical) interviewer that you're the best person for the job, you bring forth the Sales Director of Firm You, because he or she is the best suited for this particular task.

Let's take a pause and try this idea on for size. Let's pretend that you are the Sales Director of a very successful company named Firm You. You're present at a meeting selling a business or service. You are not a single person. Instead, you are a business that contains a multitude of talents, skills and viewpoints.

Can you see how this change in perspective takes the sting of anxiety and stress out of the interviewing process? Can you feel the shift that takes place within when you re-imagine the process as a sales meeting, not a nerve-wracking interview? That, in simple terms, is the essence of Interview Dynamics.

We take you through various exercises that are the cornerstones of Interview Dynamics. Each of them is meant to prepare you so thoroughly that you'll be ready with an answer to any question that is thrown at you during the interview. The cornerstones of Interview Dynamics are: -

1. Knowing yourself
2. Projecting yourself with confidence and communicating with clarity
3. The Business Plan

We briefly mentioned the various figures of authority within Firm You; now let's take a closer look at what each of them encompasses before explaining how they kick in during the interview process.

THE ASSETS THAT LIE WITHIN

To recap, Firm You (Pty) Ltd is You. The company you are hoping to land a job in is a potential customer called the Prospective Employer.

There are four important job designations within Firm You: -

1. Managing Director – The MD is the visionary who, through investment in education, training and work experience, has guided Firm You to

where it is today. As MD, he or she wants to direct the business to the next level.

2. Financial Director – He or she knows the value of your business (or your salary) and must have this figure at his or her fingertips in order to arrive at a fair deal during negotiations with the prospective employer.

3. Sales Director – The Sales Director is always on the ball. For the Sales Director, an interview is just another business meeting. He or she is the public face of Firm You, and is always "selling" on the job during the daily course of work. Let's not mistake "selling" with just being words and fluff and little else. Firm You has to back up the sales pitch of the Sales Director with a solid, outstanding performance.

4. Project Director - He or she is the one who goes all out into doing the research and the homework. The Project Director delves into the ins and outs of a potential job – analyzing the job description, the tasks and projects that make up the job, the skills, training and education required – all with the goal of matching your assets and qualifications to the job description. By verifying all that is required for the position, you can clearly show how you are able to deliver.

BUILDING THE BUSINESS OF FIRM YOU

We start with you wearing the hat of a Project Director who, in a manner of speaking, has to draft out a blueprint for a major project. Imagine a project director tasked with bidding for a project to build a bridge. He or she has to identify the assets and resources available, pinpoint strengths, weaknesses and experience of such resources, organize them into various functional teams, identify key tasks and lay out a timeline.

In this case, you're the Project Director and Firm You is your task at hand. There are three steps that you have to undertake:

- Task A: Brainstorm and jot down all your skills, experiences, extra training, your problem-solving expertise, and strengths and weaknesses relevant to the position you are applying for. This is a no-holds barred session; let go, write down everything that comes to mind. Don't edit yourself -- that comes later. At this stage, use as many pages as you need.

- Task B: Organize the mass of information from Task A into distinct categories relevant to the functions in the job description. Categories include education, skills, competencies, tasks, projects, jobs functions and so forth. This continues until all information from Task A has been neatly slotted under the various appropriate headings.

- Task C: Chunk up information from Task 2 and extract only key tasks appropriate to each heading. This is the final step in your homework as Project Director. You take only the most relevant information from each of the categories in Task B and transfer them to another page with the following important headings: education, courses, tech-skills, job functions, strengths and weaknesses, salary, questions about the job. Think of this as the final step in connecting the dots between what you have and what is required.

KNOW YOURSELF:
COMMUNICATION + CLARIFICATION + COMMUNICATION

These next exercises are to get you to thoroughly know yourself. By working through the three tasks from A to C, you are building and re-familiarizing yourself with a database of resources, competencies and skills that you already have at your disposal. Through this exercise, you'll regain confidence in who you really are and refresh your memory as to your creativity, achievements and accomplishments.

During the interview, you'll be wearing the hat of the Sales Director, who is out to sell the business of Firm You (Pty) Ltd. Having done this kind of homework, you'll be able to answer difficult and awkward questions with credibility and authority, and basically demonstrate that you have all it takes to land the job.

Having all the important bits of information at your fingertips because of the hard work put into preparation, you, as the Sales Director, are able to communicate clearly.

You will also be in a position of strength to answer with clarity, without hemming or hawing or taking awkward pauses, any questions the interviewer may ask of you.

Lastly, you will come across as a confident figure because you are well-prepared; you are able to adroitly handle any awkward questions thrown at you on any aspect of the job at hand.

REMUNERATION

You have come this far in the interview process, and now you could come undone in what is inevitably a sticky issue: how much you should be paid. No matter how well you have performed so far, this issue could be the deal-breaker if you don't put sufficient thought into your worth.

In Interview Dynamics, we provide a different take on this subject. We give you a formula, one coined by your Financial Director (it's now his or her time to step up to the plate), so you can reframe the salary negotiation not as a do-or-die situation, but as a means of getting a fair return on your output.

When you think about it, you strike a deal with someone who sells you a product or service because you think and feel you're getting a fair return on your money. Let's take this point a little further. Your Prospective Employer buys from Firm You and pays you in the form of your salary (Total Cost to Company or TCTC), in order to get desirable products and services to sell to his end customer in return for money. Naturally, he will want to make a profit on top of this cost. In order for the Prospective Employer to make a fair return and to strike a deal with you, your Financial Director values Firm You as follows: -

TCTC X 4 = Your Salary X 1 + TCTC X 3 = Profit to Prospective Employer = Fair Deal.

FROM PREP TO THE DOTTED LINE: SO WHO ARE YOU?

Now that we've covered the groundwork, there's still a little way to go before you get to sign on the dotted line. You have to be comfortable talking about yourself and polishing your storytelling skills. The more success stories you can offer, the better you show yourself as being likely to achieve equivalent success in the future. You have to be able to talk about yourself because, without fail, the question will come up "Tell us about yourself." You're certainly not boosting your hiring chances if you hesitate or respond with something unprofessional like "What do you wish to know?"

With that in mind, you have to be fully prepared to talk in detail about work that you have done in the past that made a difference to your then employer. As part of our process in Interview Dynamics, we'll guide you to coming up with concrete examples such as how you successfully closed a sale with an important customer or how you found solutions to an ongoing and expensive problem. Be conversant with your strengths and weaknesses to help your interviewer connect the dots as to why you are a winning pick for the job. This phase of the process is not as tough as it sounds because of all the prep work previously done by your Project Director.

Being asked about your mistakes is a normal thing. Do not panic, because it is in fact something that you can prepare for. Take the time right now to consider what you have done wrong. As you talk about the incident, talk about how you fixed it, how you learned from it, and how you would prevent something like that from ever happening again! This shows initiative, and it also gives your Prospective Employer an idea of how you could solve any of their problems in the future.

THE BUSINESS PLAN

Now, you turn the spotlight on the job itself. Is this project worth bidding for, so to speak? Does the job in question meet your needs? In a manner of speaking, Firm You has to analyze this opportunity, just as any business considering a potential investment would, and thus come up with a business plan. As Project Director, you have done the research and crunched the analytics. The Managing Director then weighs up whether or not this new job will take Firm You and its profitability to the next level. The Financial Director suggests the price that Firm You wants and, if everyone is in agreement, it is then up to the Sales Director to sell Firm You.

QUESTIONING THE QUESTIONER

As the interview process winds down, you may feel that you are in the home stretch. However, there is still the area where you are allowed to ask the person giving the interview any questions you have in mind. Make no mistake about it -- this is as much a test as anything else that has transpired before.

In the previous part of the interview, you were being tested to see how well you responded to stimuli. Now you are being judged on how well you are able to act independently.

Remember that, if you have done your research about the company and have the business plan at hand, you have plenty to talk about. For example, if you have noticed that the company has been very active on social media, mention it and ask if there are responsibilities, considering your ease at social marketing, which you can cover. This shows initiative, and it also allows the questioner to see how interested you are in the job.

You may choose to ask what they feel the biggest challenge of the job will be. Not only will this give you some very important information about the job, you'll also discover that it gives you a chance to tell them how you would deal with it.

Do not allow the space in the interview where you are allowed to ask questions catch you by surprise. They are watching for that because this is where many people show how unprepared or unsuitable they are. For example, if you are interviewing at a non-profit organisation and, suddenly, all you can talk about are vacation days, there's likely a mismatch there!

Do not miss out on this great opportunity to show your prospective employers how interested you are in what they do. This isn't a time when the tables are turned. In fact, it is just a shift in the form of the interview. They are still looking at you, and you still need to impress them!

FINALIZING THE INTERVIEW DYNAMICS PROCESS

Reading is all well and good, but now you need to put some physical effort into the process. With all of this preparation, which is integral throughout Interview Dynamics, you have all the raw information that you need to make a great impression at your interview. Now you need to refine it, and that starts with writing.

Whether you are most comfortable with a pen and pencil, or you are someone who is most at ease in front of a computer screen, you are now going to sit down and put your interviewing skills and writing skills to work.

Sit down, clear your head and start typing up the interview as you imagine it happening to you. Write out all of the questions that you think will be asked, and spend some time with each one. What do you think they are asking you, and what do you think they are looking for? Then, using this information, craft your responses.

Some people balk at writing line-by-line responses. They fear that it will feel rehearsed or simply trite, but the truth of the matter is that it is not as though you will be reading these things out loud to the person who is interviewing you! Instead, writing out your response will give you a strong foundation on which you can build your answers. You will know the content of what you want to say, but as the situation develops and as you gain more confidence and more mastery over what is going on, you will simply be using the original groundwork as a springboard to the right answer.

When you are preparing to sell yourself to a prospective buyer, you will find that one of the most important things that you can do is to be prepared. Once you have the information that you need, go over it again and again until you know it completely. You may think that you know your strengths and your weaknesses but, until you have been over them a few times, you will never be able to explain them to others.

Good preparation is the key to success and, not only must you have the abilities that the employer is asking for, you must also be someone who can talk about them and who can make the employer understand what you are offering. Do not fall behind simply because, after all the preparation you have done, you fall down on the delivery!

A PROFESSIONAL APPLICATION

It can often feel as if you are walking a fine line between presenting yourself as a unique individual and standing out for being too silly or too personal but, with Interview Dynamics, we show you how to walk that line with absolutely no fear at all. When you think about the fact that there may be dozens, perhaps even hundreds or thousands, of people applying for the job that you want, it is natural to get cold feet but, by applying the principles of Interview Dynamics, you have the advantage of a strong foundation to fall back on.

We show you how to create a rock-solid presentation for your application, and it is founded upon sheer professionalism. A resumé and an application get your foot in the door at the place where you want to work, but being able to demonstrate that you have a lot to bring to the table and that you have what it takes will send your name right to the top of the candidate list.

The key is to leave your ego out of it. You have done many things in your life, and you have certainly done things to be proud of. You have conquered mountains and of course you are proud of the effort that you have put in. However, the thing to remember is that the business that is speaking to you is not interested as much in how hard you work, but in seeing the results that you produce.

This is the key to professionalism and one that few people really grasp. In the quest to learn more about the business that you want to work with, get to know them. What results are they looking for? Do they want their company name to be known as a leader in green initiatives? Are they looking to make sure that they always come out on top in their field? Are they hoping to reform an image that might have been tarnished or dented in recent years?

If you want to make your application stand out, remember that it is less about you and more about the people with whom you are trying to communicate. There has never been a better time to be you, and you must show the company that you are considering why that might be.

Leave your ego at the door, and remember that your application needs to show them why they not only want you, but why they need you!

TAKING SCORE AND PRESENTING THE SALES PITCH

We are now almost at the end of the process. Just to make sure all your bases are covered, we'll score all the prep work you have done to identify what may be missing and what may need to be further supplemented. Once you're satisfied with the score, we'll move on to the last section.

As the final step, we'll run you through a self-interview where you ask questions of yourself and write down your answers to take a measure of how effectively your Sales Director is pitching your business. Are you selling your business in an efficient and professional manner? Where do you need to be refined and polished? What more do you need to know? Are you fully prepared to proceed and come through with flying colors?

By presenting yourself as a business, you are in fact able to distance yourself from the personal anxieties and insecurities that often dog an interview. Instead, you are selling a business you believe in – Firm You – and by doing so you are separating yourself from the sea of applicants and showing up as a winner!

There are multiple uses of Interview Dynamics. It is not just a process to get a new job. You can use all the steps embodied in Interview Dynamics to perform a self-assessment of your work before your annual review or, if you are lobbying for a promotion, use this same process to clearly establish why you deserve better, what additional skills and competencies you have to offer, how you have sought to improve yourself throughout the year, and how the company is going to get a fair value for your services. This process works for anyone, whether you are reporting to the financial director who answers to the board of directors or whether you are an office clerk reporting to the office manager.

Remember, you may not always be the best candidate with the most premium skills. But if you come across as being fully prepared and fully confident, you will be the most memorable and very likely the most winning candidate.

I wish you every success in selling Firm You (Pty) Ltd.

Hi, my name is Ossy Botha. I am from Johannesburg South Africa where I've worked in the recruitment industry for 32 years and counting.

Over this period of time, I have recruited and placed people in various positions and in many different companies – both large and small.

The positions which I recruit for cover a wide range of disciplines -- from senior management level to office support, administration, sales, logistics, production, technical support personnel and the like.

In a nutshell, from the front door receptionist to the back door of the business and from the bottom to the top floor.

Throughout the years, I have attended many courses, read articles on interviewing skills and gained interview techniques from the internet, all of which have proven to be very helpful.

The Interview Dynamics concept is vastly different from any existing techniques. In fact, I have not come across any material that remotely resembles what Interview Dynamics has to offer.

The reason for incorporating Interview Dynamics into your preparation is that it is a deep and thorough process during which you really get to know yourself while gaining tools and skills on how to represent yourself during an interview.

Interview Dynamics changes your perception from an applicant hoping to land the job, to that of a Company Director attending a business meeting.

Over the past years I have interviewed a countless number of people with whom I have shared the Interview Dynamics concept, all of whom have been grateful for receiving this methodology.

Therefore, I would like to share this accolade received from Savashni who was applying for a local and overseas creditor's administrator position. After our initial discussion, I walked her through the Interview Dynamics methodology.

Unfortunately, she was not invited to the prospective employer for an interview because they had just offered the opportunity to another applicant whom I had introduced to the company simply because she could begin work immediately.

However, Savashni continued to use Interview Dynamics to prepare for other job interviews as she was fully committed to the process. This is what she has to say:

"I met with Ossy in January 2014 for a position advertised for a certain company. Unfortunately I did not manage to secure an interview, but the effect of my meeting with Ossy did not end there.

I have since been to various agencies and interviews and, as of last week, I was successful in securing three jobs -- all finance related, at three different companies. That was such a surprise, from having no interviews to securing three jobs. Based on my career path, I chose the first company and will be starting with them in the 2nd week of April.

All of this was possible because I used the tips and advice I received from Ossy. I used his techniques and focused on my key achievements and abilities and put myself forward to each of my interviewers as a business, not just as an individual. His techniques really helped me to build my self-confidence.

My meeting with Ossy was really a life lesson that I shall take with me into my future. I honestly don't believe that I would have been so successful in all three interviews if I did not use Ossy's Interview Dynamic techniques.

Thank you very much. I wish Ossy and the business everything of the best for the future.

Kind Regards,
Savashni"

Should you be interested in obtaining these techniques, log onto **www.jobmasters.co.za**

Change your world. Don't miss out on achieving your career goals due to poor interviewing skills.

Thank you for reading my version of how to prepare for your forthcoming interview. The effort that you put into this concept will improve your chances of taking your business to the next level.

Control Money Before Money Controls You

K. RAJ SINGH

My aim in contributing to this book is to inspire and motivate others through sharing my experiences – both successes and failures. My hope for you is that after reading, you realize you are just as, or even more, capable of becoming successful and having financial freedom as I have had the fortune to be. Don't get me wrong; I have had to overcome multiple obstacles in order to end up where I am in life. I believe that we don't go through mishaps and failures solely to benefit ourselves, but also so that we can impart our wisdom upon the general public and benefit humanity's quality of life as a whole.

My drive and ambition stems from growing up in a single parent household with my mother and sister. Early on in life, my parents divorced and I was given the role of man of the house. I soon found that with that title came responsibility – responsibility to provide for my family, support my family, and secure a stable financial future. Throughout this time, my ambition was in the background, ever-fueling and driving my desire for more. I wanted more for my future, more for my family, but not just in a financial sense. I've heard of so many families that struggle not financially, but emotionally, because the provider was continuously absent due to their efforts to secure a stable lifestyle for their family. I didn't want to impart that emotional burden on my family. I wanted to be there for them and not just function as their savings account or an invisible man who allows them to live a comfortable life. I wanted to be there for my sister's graduation, or my child's first steps and first words. I wanted to be present.

Being a good person and being successful are not mutually exclusive characteristics, but neither do they come hand in hand. You can be a genuinely good human being in terms of honesty and generosity, but not accomplished in terms of achieving your career goals. In order to become who I wanted to be for my family, I had to learn how to be both the best and most successful person I had the potential to be. To do this, I attended multiple seminars and workshops on personal development, investing, and financial success. To this day, I still continue to learn and grow as a person with every day I live, but one seminar has had a significant impact on my financial life, specifically. This was Peak Potentials' Millionaire Mind Intensive by T. Harv Eker (now called New Peaks' Millionaire Mind Experience*). The Millionaire Mind Intensive seminar taught me not to just wonder why life is the way it is and imagine my position in life as static, but to start asking myself how I could change my financial blueprint and future. And that's exactly what I did.

I am now in a global mastermind group with New Peaks and feel blessed to have been able to spend time with the CEO, Adam Markel, who is also author of the book Pivot. I've visited him in his home in California, where we spent hours brainstorming ideas and solutions for our businesses, while also making time for fun and giving back to a worthy cause with our time and physical labor. The dedication that Mr. Markel and the rest of his team put into their company is wondrous and admirable. I, along with countless other people, have taken many of the courses and retreats they offer – my favorite being the Enlightened Warrior Training Camp. The name alone says a lot about the focus of the retreat as becoming an enlightened warrior means to conquer oneself.

As I mentioned before, I wanted to figure out a way to be financially successful but also be present for my family. The best way I have found to do this was to delegate and relinquish some control. For some people this may be hard, especially the types that are perfectionists and relish the ability to oversee every detail of any operation. But in order for me to have enough free time to spend with my family and loved ones, I had to realize that a significant amount of the work I did myself could be distributed and done by other people. I began to hire others to do the more routine work I had grown accustomed to doing myself and although at first glance this seemed like a big initial investment, I soon reaped its benefits. Not having to do the work of multiple people allowed me to focus on the more complex aspects of the projects I was working on and with greater focus came increased levels of productivity. That's when the successes started rolling in.

None of the headway I made after bringing in others to help would have been possible if I hadn't realized the importance of continued education, even after obtaining my Bachelor's Degree. This doesn't necessarily have to mean taking online classes or auditing courses at your local college – it can be as simple as reading an article on a topic you don't know much about or taking a weekend and attending a seminar on smart investing. Having a vast store of a variety of information allows you to be creative in your problem solving and future planning, as you can take multiple viewpoints when looking at the situations you find yourself in. "Knowledge is power" isn't a famous quote just because the sound of the words is aurally appealing; there is innate truth in those three words, dating back to 1597 in Sir Francis Bacon's Meditationes Sacrae. As you can see, this book isn't just about investing in stocks or bonds; rather it's about investing in yourself – your education, your future, and your success. To take it a step further, I believe knowledge, when applied, is power. Warren Buffet, the biggest investor of our time, says: "The best investment you can make is an investment in yourself… The more you learn, the more you'll earn." I've noticed throughout my life that wealthy people tend to always have extensive libraries in their homes and I firmly believe there is a correlation between their success and the importance they put on accumulating knowledge. Knowledge, and the ability of correctly applying it, are the greatest assets in the world because the dividends are infinite.

*As a thank you for purchasing this book, I am offering a scholarship certificate for you and a family member to attend the 3-day Millionaire Mind Experience Seminar as my complimentary guests. Valued at $2,590 – free for a limited time! Go to www.thepassiveincomebook.com

THE LAW OF ATTRACTION

The law of attraction ultimately boils down to the idea that "like attracts like." In a way, our thoughts are made up of energy, just as we are, and whether our thoughts are positive or negative can determine whether we encounter positive or negative experiences. The idea of similar energy types attracting each other, also known as the law of attraction, was brought to fame and popularity through Rhonda Byrne's book-turned-movie, The Secret. I was blessed to come across this book at a pivotal point in my life and owe most of my beliefs to the lessons I took from reading it. I truly believe it to be the single most powerful and impactful piece of literature I have studied. When I met the greatest motivational speaker, Anthony Robbins*, I learned that all of us have a vibrational energy, and in order to succeed, we need to increase our energy levels to the maximum we can obtain. The more energy we have, the more of what we want from the universe we can attract. You can think of it in terms of gravity – bigger bodies of matter have bigger gravitational pulls, and ultimately attract larger amounts of mass. The sun is a good example of this. Surrounded by eight planets, a dwarf planet, and countless asteroids, the sun is a giant orb, pulsing of energy and attracting an incredible amount of matter towards it. We should all try to draw as much positive energy towards ourselves as possible.

An efficient way to attract favorable energy is to actively maintain a positive attitude every day. I cannot stress enough how important I have found having a positive attitude to be. Especially since we live in a world where negative happens all around us, this may initially be harder than it seems but with conscious effort, staying positive can become habit. To help you visualize this, I want you to imagine a field of dirt. Without doing anything or putting in any effort, grass and weeds will take it over and destroy its potential. However, by planting your own crops and nurturing them with fertile soil and water, you can eventually end up with a bountiful field full of fruits or vegetables. With effort, the positive has overcome the default negative. In this same way, actively trying to maintain a positive attitude can help you eliminate the negative that regrettably encompasses the world.

A more tangible way to do this in your daily life is to listen to personal development and motivational audio books in your spare time. I used to use the time I spent commuting to work to do this; I even called my car my "University on Wheels." No matter where I was going, I was always able to feel as if I'd done something productive, other than driving from point

A to point B. If audio books aren't up your alley, you could also opt for the real paper version of the books. Reading every night before bed has become a deeply embedded habit for me, and I regard it as a habit everyone should develop. Most people spend their last minutes before sleep watching the news on TV, something full to the brim with negativity. "If it bleeds, it leads" is a common phrase that comes to mind when we think about the news – is that something really the last thing we want to be exposed to before sleeping? Our mind will slowly fade away from consciousness as we fall asleep, but our subconscious is still processing all of the violence and blood we witnessed through the TV. I equate watching the news before bed with letting someone come into your home and throw garbage everywhere right before you leave the house. Don't let something as negative as a newscast filled with misfortune and violence fill your mind right before sleep. Alternatively, think about if you were to just read a few pages of a motivational book before going to bed – the last words you experience before sleep are now something positive and propelling. You wake up feeling refreshed and energized the next morning, ready to tackle whatever challenges you may face that day.

A good tactic I have found for achieving success and a positive attitude is to find a person who is successful in the way you want to be and to study them. As I mentioned before, continuing education is an important part of achieving your goals, and studying people is yet another way you can learn to improve. I've had countless mentors over the years and even a life coach to help me through the happy and more complicated times. Each of these people has impacted my life in different ways, as every one of them had different experiences and types of knowledge to offer. I consciously recognize that without these people, I would be nowhere near the place where I am today. I am also able to realize that not only have these people helped me get to where I am now, but also my past mistakes have been integral to my success.

I firmly stand by the idea that we are all in the right place at the right time. Even though things may seem difficult at that specific time, or you may fail once or twice or several times, everything that happens to you is meant to happen. No matter the situation, there is always a lesson you can learn from your experiences.

Your income will never exceed your self-image of how great you perceive yourself to be, therefore you must grow your self-image alongside self-improvement to feel truly worthy of a greater income. In order to better visualize my goals, I created a vision board. A vision board can be something as simple as a poster with pictures of things you want in your future, regardless of what facet of life they pertain to. I love staring at my vision board and feeling excited about living in that reality. I encourage everyone to ponder over their vision board every day and visualize living that life in the present so you can attract it. It's a rewarding feeling that I can't properly put into words when you're able to start watching yourself achieve those goals and subsequently replacing them with new dreams. Some of the things I've achieved from my vision board are owning a new Mercedes Benz, meeting Billionaire Sir Richard Branson* at the iconic Playboy Mansion, meeting Mogul P. Diddy*, having a library for others to learn from, invited to Tai Lopez's $16 Million Mansion in Beverly Hills*, owning different passive income businesses I'll discuss later in the chapter, and so many more.

Going along with the idea that exuding positive energy attracts more positive energy, I believe that gratitude is one of the most powerful forces of the universe. Being grateful in life attracts more things to be grateful for. I believe if the ability to feel gratitude is not learned on the way up, then it will surely be learned on the way down. To make sure I have agency in expressing and being aware of the things I'm grateful for, I often write in my Gratitude Journal before I go to sleep at night. Essentially it is a list of all the things I feel blessed to have in life overall, specifically for that day, and specifically in that moment.

Unfortunately, most people are used to thinking about all the things in life they are unhappy about. They subsequently focus on and put passion into those things to try and fix them which is a recipe for more disaster. Rather than counting their blessings, they're counting their problems. Once you find a way to deliberately focus on all of your blessings, more of them will come to you and you will ultimately be happier in life. As I like to say, "the Pessimist may be more accurate, but the Optimist lives longer and happier."

A way that I have found to remain positive and focused on my blessings is having sessions with my life coach, whom I've had for over a decade now. Our sessions have consisted of a half an hour phone call every 2 weeks for over the last 10 years. My life coach, Dr. Elena Pezzini, helps me to set realistic goals and holds me accountable to them. She also is always making sure all areas of my life are in balanced harmony with each other and steers me in the right direction if I am lacking in an area of health, wealth, family, relationships, business, sociality, or spirituality. She always reminds me how important it is to celebrate my successes.

Alongside Dr. Pezzini, I have a sort of personal advisory board I go to on different subjects. In addition to paying for my professional life coach, I have a vocal coach for singing, spiritual advisors, specialty business mentors, and a therapist, all of whom I consult with regularly. A key point here is to pay for it – especially with life and business advisors, you get what you pay for, and when you have some skin in the game you value it more. If you are the smartest person in the room, then you're in the wrong room. You are a product of your environment and surrounding yourself with those who you perceive as more intelligent or successful will cause you to strive to be more like them. Swami Paramhansa Yogananda gave us the aphorism, "environment is stronger than will power." The Ramayan scripture states that when you are surrounded with a certain company you will then be like that company. Is your surrounding harvesting your growth?

*See my pictures with Anthony Robbins, teachers featured in The Secret, Sir Richard Branson, Tai Lopez, etc. at www.thepassiveincomebook.com

MY PAST REAL ESTATE SUCCESS STORIES

Fortunately for me, my success story featured on a National Cable & Television broadcast on the Cash Flow Generator infomercial* when I earned a six-figure profit after only my first year in real estate. This, in part, allowed me to jumpstart my success in the real estate industry and eventually at the height of my involvement in the field, I had managed hundreds of tenants across multiple buildings. In the years preceding and following this time, I learned many lessons. The most important ones I learned, though, involved how to compromise and deal with people who weren't always willing to meet in the middle. No matter what field you work in or where you live in the world, you will always come across people who truly believe that they are always right in their opinions or mindsets. Being exposed to this type of personality so early on in my professional life allowed me to use the tactics I gained throughout my property managing days to more efficiently deal with my future bosses, employees, and investors. People-managing skills are amongst the most relevant that you can gain.

Overseeing numerous buildings also meant constantly having to maintain the infrastructure and quality of dwellings. Often enough, a new problem arose – burst pipes, new carpeting needed, leaky ceilings – you name it, I probably dealt with it. These problems had me in consistent contact with contractors, plumbers, electricians, and handymen in general. A majority of the contractors I dealt with were exceedingly unreliable, and this caused me many a setback in getting my apartments move-in-ready. The more time my properties were vacant, the more money I lost. Thankfully I had some financial leeway because of the income my other properties brought in, but for someone with not as many properties, an inefficient contractor could mean the difference between a successful investment in a rental property or a failure. Take your time in choosing whom you work with in maintaining or renovating your building, and always budget for possible money lost if the project takes longer than expected (which it always does).

Unfortunately, alongside difficult tenants and fickle contractors, I also had to deal with lawsuits. Fraud, discrimination in screening applicants, and physical injury on the property are among the most common problems I had to deal with. Fortunately, I ran my properties with the utmost care and honesty, so none of the lawsuits I personally encountered ever succeeded in their intentions. Yet another lesson I can impart upon you relates to that – be honest in your dealings and avoid shortcuts. Even though these things may seem like they provide an immediate benefit, in the long run they are detrimental to your success. In the late 60s, psychologist Walter Mischel led a series of experiments on delayed gratification, which were subsequently named the Stanford Marshmallow Experiments. In these experiments, a young child was given the choice between being able to eat one marshmallow immediately or waiting 10-15 minutes and being able to eat two marshmallows. Decades later, Mischel followed up with the children from the original studies and measured multiple facets of success. Ultimately, the children who were able to delay gratification for a bigger reward down the line were more successful in multiple areas of life, including both professional success and being able to maintain a healthy lifestyle. You can see from this study that success is correlated to one's ability to see into the future and realize that maybe the quickest reward is not the best.

*See the Infomercial video clip at www.thepassiveincomebook.com

MY PAST INVESTMENT HISTORY

Although investing can have its advantages, it can also be harmful if you aren't careful or attentive with your investments. It also isn't an immediate profit that you earn if you choose to stick with it for the long run, rather than day trading or choosing more short-term investments. Look at the stock market – it varies day-to-day, month-to-month, and year-to-year. Some stocks can increase generously in the matter of weeks while others can take much longer to see the same increase in return. There is no guarantee, either, that you will make money off of your investment, regardless of how accomplished your investment manager is. Companies are unpredictable, as there are so many things that can contribute to their value, and sometimes despite your best efforts and time spent researching, an investment can go the opposite way intended.

A few companies that I invested in ultimately ended up shutting down before I could cash out my funds, and I had to quickly rebalance my finances when faced with these unexpected losses. These setbacks taught me to more carefully weigh the risks and benefits of the investment portfolios I considered, even if it took up a little more of my time than I intended. I viewed these losses as obstacles I had to overcome and didn't let them discourage me from future investments, if a seemingly profitable one came across my path.

Another business venture that aided in my financial success was my involvement in network marketing businesses, also known as multi-level marketing. You've probably heard of a few of these – Amway is one of the better-known network marketing businesses I was heavily involved in, as well as Prepaid Legal Services (now called Legal Shield), and Javita. The basic idea of these types of companies is that an individual buys in to the company and can earn commission on the products that they end up selling. This type of "employment" allows you to be flexible in your hours, work from home, and essentially be your own boss. They typically require a minimal initial investment to get a sample of the product you're selling and to gain a feel for how to market it when you start selling to other people. This type of business venture usually attracts people who are looking for flexible employment and if you can dedicate enough time and effort, it can end up being quite the lucrative option. The personal development and leadership ability gained here in their proven system are priceless.

My father would say to me that you should have 3 types of people in your life: 1) someone greater than you to learn from, 2) someone at your level to exchange ideas with, and 3) someone younger than you to teach what you've learned. Network Marketing provides an opportunity for all 3 with your up-line, down-line, and sideline people.

DISCOVER YOUR PASSION

An easy way to discover what you're truly passionate about is to take a step back and look at your hobbies. Hobbies are what you choose to do in your free time and are things you genuinely enjoy, rather than being something you feel obligated to do because it provides for your family or allows you to lead an extravagant lifestyle. You will be most successful in endeavors that you're passionate about since working towards your goals won't seem like work.

Unfortunately, sometimes your hobbies don't necessarily match up with what kind of income you need in life. That's when you try your best to find a career field that you can be successful in, while also making time to do the things you truly enjoy. Maintaining a consistent effort towards having one or two interests outside of work will help keep you feeling satisfied with where you are in life.

Another way to work towards becoming the most successful person you can be is looking at why you do the things you do. I've noticed throughout my life that as long as you're doing something for the right reasons, things will generally fall in your favor. Why you're doing something ultimately determines how you do it. If you start something with good intentions, you will put in the effort necessary for making sure your goals come to fruition. On the other hand, if you work towards something but with the wrong intentions, you may still become successful, although there is a smaller chance of that and your achievements may not feel as satisfying as if why you did that was for a purer reason. This is yet another reason why you should look at your hobbies and try your hardest to find a career that matches up with them. If what you end up doing for the rest of your life is something you're truly passionate about, then you will have become the most successful person you can be.

For me, my passions have to do mainly with the arts and performing in front of an audience of thousands of people locally and internationally. My favorite quote is from the movie Braveheart "Everyone dies, but not everyone truly lives." I feel truly alive when I sing with my band on stage, act on stage for charity, emcee events, and even do TV/Radio interviews. All of these were done alongside my investments in the stock market, FOREX market, and real estate, and they helped me maintain a feeling of being creative, something I truly cherish. Even though I didn't make a full-time career out of any of my hobbies, I was still able to pursue them because I found a way to run my business efficiently and have enough free time. Without a way to express my creative side, I most likely would have failed at most of the goals I tried to achieve career-wise as I would have felt confined in a world where I wasn't able to be completely myself.

I also derive satisfaction from contributing back to my community or the world I live in through charity work. To some people this can mean writing a check for some non-profit organization, while for others it can mean being directly involved with the charity through volunteering or being on the board. Some have the time for the latter while for most all they can contribute is a small monetary donation. I love the Sai Baba quote that says "Hands that serve mankind are holier than lips that pray". I find as long as I'm able to lend a helping hand in some way, I feel as if I've done some good with my life. However, I do advise you take caution with the charities you choose to invest in, as some don't actually give back as much as the general public thinks they do.

Luckily enough for me, even though it may have happened upon me later in life than I preferred, I found something I was genuinely passionate about that I could also make money off of. That was investing on a diverse scale. I loved the continual education that was required of investing. I always had to know what was going on in the market or in foreign economies so that I could try and predict which of my investments was going to become profitable, or which ones I should just cut my losses with. I then started hiring people smarter than me. I ended up loving it so much that I chose to start my own private investment club and became the go-to guy for people that wanted ideas about passive income investing. I have faith and hope that everyone in life will eventually be able to find an opportunity to be successful and happy like I have, even if it may cross your path when you least expect it.

PASSIVE INCOME

Passive income is part of the idea of unearned income; essentially, it is income that is received on a consistent basis with minimal effort put in to manage and maintain it. You can receive unearned or passive income from things such as pensions, inheritance, and property income, which don't require any active effort to profit from. These types of earnings are what people typically become wealthy from, rather than the salary they earn from their day jobs. Instead of living directly off of their earnings from their day jobs, many people can cut down on their daily expenses and use those savings to invest in opportunities that allow them to earn a passive income.

The most common ways to earn passive income are through rental and investment income. Rental income initially is not purely passive income, as the initial down payment and maintenance of the property can require a lot of time and effort depending on the state and quality of the building or buildings you choose to purchase. Even after this initial investment, there is still a consistent effort that needs to be put in for rental properties to maintain profitability. You have to collect checks from every tenant each month (which may not always go through) and deal with a multitude of problems that arise from difficult tenants or neighbors, or even from the infrastructure of the building itself. Rental income, however, is more a passive income than your day job, and can sometimes even be more profitable if managed in an efficient way.

In contrast, investment income is on the opposite spectrum of passive income and requires little effort after the initial investment to start earning profit. However, sometimes investing necessitates quite a large chunk of money to begin earning even a small percentage of gain. Looking at just profiting from dividends, which are payments made by a corporation to its shareholders, to make even $1,000 a year with a 4% annual dividend payout (a pretty hefty payout) you have to invest $25,000. In cases like these, it's best to do your research beforehand and find which companies are slotted to be the most profitable in the next year, as they use a fraction of their retained earnings as dividends to shareholders. The more profit a company earns, the more it can pay out to its shareholders.

There are other ways you can earn passive income through investing, too. You can trade commodities, stocks, currencies on the foreign exchange market (FOREX), securities, and even precious metals. I hire FOREX traders who I know that leverage my time so that I don't have to trade myself, or monitor the global news reports constantly. Each of these options has their advantages and drawbacks, but they are all considered a type of passive income. One of the more frequently chosen of the aforementioned options is investing in a mutual fund, which is professionally managed and pools money from multiple investors to purchase securities. This type of investment is most useful in planning for retirement, as it has a decreased amount of risk compared to investing in individual securities since a fund typically holds a diverse portfolio of securities. If one of the securities in the fund doesn't do well, chances are at least a few others did well enough to make up for the loss attributable to that one security. However, mutual funds come with fees when you buy and sell shares and are already "pre-packaged." This means you don't have as much freedom to customize your investment portfolio as you would have investing in individual securities yourself.

Another way I have found to earn passive income is through tax lien certificates. A lien is a type of security over a property to ensure that the owner pays back any debt or obligation they owe to the lien holder. A tax lien certificate, specifically, is for when a property has a lien placed upon it due to unpaid property taxes. They ultimately represent the right to foreclose on a property when there is failure of property tax payments. These certificates can be auctioned off to investors, who pay the amount of taxes owed on the property in order to then gain the right to collect the unpaid taxes from the owners plus the current rate of interest on tax lien certificates. These rates can range anywhere from 5 to 36 percent and the property owner has a period of 6 months to 3 years to pay back the taxes and interest. If the owner fails to do so by the end of the redemption period, then the lien holder is allowed to start foreclosure proceedings and take ownership of the property. Either way, with careful consideration of which tax lien certificates you choose to buy, you could earn a fair amount of passive income. However, you must figure out what your responsibilities are concerning obtaining ownership of the lien – in some states, you are required to send multiple letters at different time points notifying the owners that you now own the lien and if they fail to repay their taxes, you can foreclose on their property. Some even have expiration dates where if you don't initiate foreclosure proceedings within a certain time after the redemption period, you no longer have the right to the property. All in all, tax lien certificates have the potential to be highly profitable if you can do the research required of them.

A less well-known method of generating passive income is through owning or leasing ATM machines. The way to make a passive income through this is with the service fee that most ATMs impose upon the user. Typically, these range anywhere from $2-$5 and with each transaction on the machine, that is what you end up earning. Although it may seem like a miniscule amount at first glance, imagine if just 10 people a day used your machine. At the low end of service fees, that still equates to $600 a month with you essentially doing nothing. First off, you have to make the decision to either purchase or lease an ATM machine. Even though purchasing an ATM requires a larger initial investment, it is ultimately less expensive than leasing a machine, as you own it outright rather than having to pay a monthly fee to use and profit from it. There are some legal hoops that you may have to jump through, though, such as registering the ATM machine with your county clerk if you plan on running it under a business' name. After you ensure you have all the proper licenses, you can start placing the ATM machines in carefully picked locations, which is ultimately what matters most when trying to profit from this type of venture. You want to guarantee that your ATM is placed in an area that receives enough foot traffic and is far away enough from a bank that it is more convenient for people to withdraw money from your ATM than the bank.

Finally, the last approach I'll mention here to generating passive income that I have personally done and can suggest is through product sourcing or drop shipping. Product sourcing is a way to sell items on eBay or Amazon where the sellers never actually handle the item and instead it is sent directly from the warehouse to the buyer. The sellers of the products purchase in bulk from the warehouse, but the warehouse holds the items for the seller and then ships it out when a buyer purchases a unit. By buying in bulk, the seller is able to receive a discount on the item, which they can then choose to sell full price to the buyer. This is essentially where your profit comes from through product sourcing. There are some disadvantages to this method though – most notably is the fact that drop shippers frequently run out of stock of their more popular items, which the seller doesn't find out until after they sell the item and notify the supplier that it needs to be shipped. This results in bad feedback for your store on eBay, and can decrease the amount of traffic you end up getting. In addition, there has recently been a rise in drop shippers exporting directly from China – essentially drop shippers are now directly selling their product on eBay themselves. This is a difficult market to enter specifically on eBay, as shoppers on this website are typically looking to strike a bargain, while you're looking to make a profit. Furthermore, some suppliers don't offer the true wholesale price on their products when you're buying on the minimum side of a bulk order. However, if you're able to establish a satisfying professional relationship with your drop shipper, and ensure that you're getting a real wholesale price, then this type of venture could be profitable.

PRIVATE INVESTMENT CLUBS

In order to benefit my friends, family, and business partners as much as possible, I started a private investment club to educate them using the experience I've gained in over the past decade. The diversity of ventures I've pursued and achieved success in makes me a unique and extensive expert on passive income. Through all of my trials and errors, I've finally figured out ways to make money work for me, rather than me working for money. I want to be able to share that knowledge with as many people as possible, which is why I decided to write this book.

If you are an accredited investor or a sophisticated investor and get accepted into a private investment club, it truly can be a passive investment – you don't need to work to earn any profit. On my website, www.thepassiveincomebook.com, you can read testimonials and referrals from multiple different people who have chosen to learn smart investing ideas and strategies with me. Like me, they're able to spend less time trying to earn money and worrying about it, and more time living a passion-filled life.

Additionally, I work with a group of commercial investors that invest in multi-family apartment building units in emerging markets and help people get a higher than average rate of return secured by real estate in the USA. I've learned about this type of commercial investing directly from Real Estate Guru David Lindahl and his mentorship program. There are so many cash flow and equity position opportunities available to someone as a private lender. Private loans can be loaned to a real estate investor and secured by real estate for rehabilitation projects, flips, or rental holdings. Private loan investors are given a first, or a second mortgage, that secures their legal interest in the property and secures their investment. "Secured" means that their money is secured by an asset, which in this case is the real estate property.

Many people don't realize that they can even invest their retirement income into real estate and other investments themselves, tax-free. You can roll it over and not get charged any penalties with a self-directed IRA. This can be an incredible way to leave a legacy for generational wealth.

RISKS, CAUTION, AND SAFETY

Like with any new adventure, there is inherent risk in investing your money in the ways I've previously mentioned. With investing, there are two basic types of risk – systematic and unsystematic. Systematic is a type of risk that you are unable to avoid when investing and it can affect a broad spectrum of assets. A good example of a systematic risk would be an important political event that could possibly influence the entire market. On the other hand, unsystematic risk, or specific risk, only affects a small number of assets. For example, if union workers from the port were to strike, then only stocks for companies that dealt with that port would be affected. Thankfully though, unlike systematic risk, you can protect yourself from unsystematic risk through diversification. The more diverse an investment portfolio you have, the more you can ensure that a drop in one stock doesn't equate to a drop in your entire portfolio, since you have different kinds of stocks that can make up for that loss. However, there is a tradeoff between risk and return – higher risk stocks typically have a higher payout while lower risk stocks tend to have a lower return. This is where you have to ask yourself, how much are you willing to gamble? Do you have the freedom to take a loss or are you still too early on in your financial journey to afford that potential loss? I want you to use the lessons from this book to be able to get yourself to a point where you feel comfortable occasionally taking those risks to get a higher payout. As long as you don't continuously invest in high-risk stocks or securities and make smart investments, you could have the opportunity to receive a high return.

I do want to caution you though. No matter how much you diversify your portfolio, the risk of investing will never be zero. You can, however, reduce it as much as possible through diversification. This doesn't just mean making sure to invest in different types of companies, but also different types of investment vehicles. There are stocks, mutual funds, real estate, foreign currency, and bonds, among other things. Choosing multiple vehicles across various industries ensures that if one takes a dive, it's more than likely that your other investments are safe and sound. A not well-known way to diversity your portfolio to reduce risk is to also vary the risk of your investments. To minimize risk, you don't have to commit yourself to only choosing blue chip stocks or other types of vehicles with very low risk. If you pick investments with varying rates of return, you can help guarantee that a high return will make up for any losses in other industries or vehicles.

If you feel like you don't have enough free time to initially commit to diversifying your own portfolio, you can always trust a professional to cultivate your portfolio for you, or invest your money in an already-created and vetted portfolio. This chapter has been all about how to make money work for you so that you have financial freedom, and as I said before, a good way to start is to delegate and get educated. So why don't you take that next step? Start investing and share with me your personal success stories and breakthroughs. Contact us today to learn more about our informational products and seminars.

To read more about K. Raj Singh's experiences and wisdom, get his newest book titled "Control $, Before $ Controls You: Finding Your Passion Through Passive Income" and visit www.thepassiveincomebook.com

KEEP YOUR JOB & GET PROMOTED ...GUARANTEED

Take Control of Your Career In Just 7 Steps

Frantz Forestal

There are a lot of books about the job market —getting a job, losing a job, balancing life and a job, and so on — but there's little to no practical help on keeping your job in a constantly changing world. No one tells you how to take charge of your career and steer it in the direction you want it to go.

Simply said, do you want to be the passenger or the driver in your career?

A passenger goes along doing the job as assigned. He or she assumes that things will go on that way forever. Unfortunately, the world doesn't work that way anymore. You can be in a job for years, only to find that the skills needed have changed, or the job isn't relevant anymore and is being eliminated. Unless you have prepared yourself for a change — seen it coming as it were —you will find yourself out of work, looking for the first job you can get (rather than getting your career back on track).

If you've been a passenger up to now, don't worry. There are things you can do to make sure this never happens to you. More than that: instead of getting fired you can likely get an increase in pay within six months or a year.

A driver, on the other hand, is always watching the road ahead. He or she looks left and right, to see what others in the company are doing, and builds relationships with the right people. A driver also keeps an eye out for changes and trends in the marketplace and learns new skills at every appropriate opportunity.

Putting yourself in the driver's seat may sound difficult, but it doesn't have to be that hard. And it doesn't have to be complicated. There's a straight line to success in any field and, when you create the path to be followed based on the business environment that you're in, you are sure to have created the right road for you. There's no way you're not going to have a good opportunity and be able to grab it.

It doesn't take a Human Relations (HR) manager or a recruiter to show you the way. Achieving your goals is a much more practical matter than most "professional" advice addresses. (Keep in mind, though, that HR people and recruiters can be helpful when you are following your path.) There are proven actions you can take that will put you on the right road and keep you on a straight path to a successful career. Here are the seven steps you need to take to guarantee — and improve — your place in the company.

1. SET UP YOUR FOUNDATION

Learn everything you can about the responsibilities and tasks associated with your job. Get better at them and stay on top of new techniques and tools by taking courses or using self-help books when needed. Be consistent in your strong performance of those responsibilities.

Behave properly while you're working. That means, dress for the next level up, be friendly and helpful (without overdoing it) and act as if you are happy to be there. Position yourself appropriately: If you act like an asset, you will be perceived as an asset.

Become friends with "the right people," both co-workers and managers who can be helpful in your career. Be someone they can trust and count on. Become the go-to person for what you do and explain just enough so that people know they don't know as much as you do about the subject.

2. KNOW WHERE YOUR JOB IS GOING

Another part of doing your job properly is making sure you know where that job is going. Start by asking yourself these questions:

- Is my job fulfilling the needs of today's marketplace?
- If not, what responsibilities or skills would prepare me to serve my clients or customers better?
- Is there an opportunity to create a new position, to meet a need or take advantage of an opportunity that most people don't yet see?
- How might my job change in the near future?
- Will my position even be here in the next five years? Ten years?

- If not, is it time to change careers?

I've benefited from doing this in my own job. I've had great success as a system accountant, something that didn't exist six or seven years ago. No one could have even written the job description in those days, but I saw that there was a problem that needed fixing and made sure that I acquired the necessary skills to fulfill that need as soon as I quickly as I could do so.

Specifically, in those days you were either an IT guy or an accountant. As accounting software became increasingly more important to conducting business, a need arose for someone who could bridge the two positions. (Financial software is mainly about how the database has been built, and how the numbers within it are linked together in different tables or with other databases.) Technical problems were a nightmare because, if you asked an IT person to fix some issues, his or her work might mess up the numbers for the accountant. What was really needed was an accountant who knew the software, so I became one.

3. DON'T PROCRASTINATE, BE PROACTIVE

Once I identified that opportunity, I didn't wait for a potential employer to come looking. I took the initiative, and contacted a recruiter to find out if there were positions available. I also asked about what I would need to do to be ready when a job came up. In other words, I made my interest and intentions known to someone who knew the market better than I did and could be of help to me.

A month or two later, the recruiter called and said that Microsoft® was offering a free class, with certification. The recruiter went on to say that, if I got this certification, he could send me out for a specific position. The software was new, Microsoft was promoting it heavily and, in just a few months, I had a new job. I was a leader in my area, among the first to know and use what has become a standard tool in my market. That made me highly desirable. I was able to negotiate the terms of my employment and even got a signing bonus.

The point of my story is simple. I made my job happen. I knew there was an unfulfilled need, made sure I was aware that there was new software coming and asked the right people for help early on. I dominated the job market because I put myself in the driver's seat.

4. BE A SQUEAKY WHEEL, MAKE YOUR INTENTIONS KNOWN

One of the most important techniques of negotiation is to ask for what you want. No one can read your mind, and bosses don't go around giving out raises or promotions just for the fun of it. Actively pursue the outcome you desire. Make your wishes known and ensure that your manager — and his or her manager — know that you deserve to be rewarded for your accomplishments and achievements. If you've set up a strong foundation, they will understand how valuable you are to the company.

Be realistic in your expectations of how quickly that raise or promotion might occur — these things don't happen overnight — but don't let someone else put you off with promises. Don't accept silence or let your manager ignore you. It may feel like you are being too aggressive but, at some point, if your manager hasn't done anything about your request, you will need to wake him up.

Don't threaten, but make it clear that you are thinking about leaving in the next six months or a year if you don't get what you want. Reiterate your accomplishments and remind him of your value.

5. KNOW YOUR REAL WORTH

You are not just valuable because of what you've already done. There will be financial repercussions if you leave, so you need to know what it will cost the company to replace you. Let's say you make $100,000 a year and decide to leave your job tomorrow. How much money will it take to fill your position?

Well, how long will it take for your manager to replace you? First, there's likely to be a two month process in which he has to request and receive permission from management and HR to fill the position, interview candidates, choose his favorites and have them meet management. Once an offer gets made, there is a period of time for the candidate to accept, give notice and be able to start. It could take four months by the time that new person is up to speed.

So, right away, there is a significant expense to the company if you move on. It could cost up to half your annual salary — in this case, $50,000 — to let you leave. Compare that to the 10% — or even 20% — increase you might be asking for and you can see how compelling a story there is to keeping you happy in your current position.

6. BE PREPARED

At some point, if you haven't received a positive response from those higher up, you will need to consider moving on. Start exploring other job opportunities, ensure that your Curriculum Vitae (CV) is current and pull together a portfolio of your accomplishments. Include any positive emails you've received, relevant certifications, a summary of the projects you've started and other materials that will help build a strong selling message.

You can and should go out for more than one job at a time. Keep looking for better and better opportunities. That's a powerful technique for moving your career ahead. Also, when you meet up with a recruiter, remember that your challenge is not to get the job offered, but to evaluate the opportunity and decide if it is right for you. When you identify a job worth pursuing, remember your worth. Stay in the driver's seat and don't be afraid to negotiate or even say no if the terms are not to your liking.

7. USE YOUR LEVERAGE

Once you have another opportunity, use it to its full advantage. Don't just close the door on your current employer. Dangle your new opportunity in front of your manager like you would a piece of candy in front of a child you want to behave. If you've built a strong foundation and been performing well, it is likely that your manager will not want you to go. He or she will likely think through the situation and talk to HR or higher management about making a counteroffer. If there is a counteroffer, give it serious consideration. Consider the pros and cons of each position and make your decision based on what's best for your long term career.

There's actually one more step you might want to consider.

8. ASK FOR HELP

The seven steps above are proven strategies for taking control of your own career. However, there may be times when you want advice on how to handle a specific situation. Don't be shy about asking for help.

If you are on LinkedIn — and you should be — ask a general question, or look up someone you know who might have experienced a similar situation. Better still, search out website communities like **www.getabigraiseguaranteed.com**, the online resource I founded for just this purpose. You'll be able to read about what others have successfully done within their own companies, or how they determined it was time to move on. Plus, it is a great place to share what's worked for you and a major resource for networking among others in your field.

The Vegan Lifestyle Solution

Make the connection between your diet and your purpose

Dagmar Schoenrock

When I was asked to write a chapter for The Authorities book series, my first thought was, "Me, an authority? I'm a compassionate vegan, not a scientist, not a nutritionist, nor do I have a Ph.D." Nonetheless, I realized that there is no authority outside oneself. I am my own authority on the life experiences that I've had, ones that took me from bison farmer to vegan. This transition was clearly a life lesson, showing me that I need to trust myself — to be my own authority. With this in mind, I am grateful to have the opportunity to share with you some of the facts that helped me return to my true vegan state of being.

Every day, in fact, I'm filled with love and gratitude for the many privileges I've been blessed with. My gratitude list is long and it begins with my parents. Thanks to them, I was raised in a country with many civil liberties, a solid economic base and a peaceful society. This wasn't by accident. I was graced with this life because my parents left their homeland and immigrated to the Canadian prairies for the sake of their children. They wanted us to grow up in a free society and live in peace, safe from the political unrest in Europe. From an early age, I knew and appreciated the value of protecting others, sacrificing for others, and peace.

This awareness played a role in how I lived my life even as a child. I would bring home stray cats and dogs, baby birds that had fallen out of their nests, or turtles trying to cross the road, asking my parents to help me reunite them with their mothers. In school, I brought home bullied classmates until the students intimidating them passed by, and they could safely walk home to their own mothers. In college, I participated in fundraising efforts for various charities to eradicate illnesses or poverty. Later, I became a Big Sister and continued with fundraising for various organizations. When I became a parent, I continued my peaceful efforts by donating to environmental and human rights groups, supporting our local green candidate in the elections, and becoming a Girl Guides leader.

I don't believe this involvement in my community makes me unique; I believe this is what connects me to all of you. Like most people, I have a goal to contribute, in some small way and through some small action, to a free and peaceful society where we can all live in harmony and peace. Regardless of our level of contribution to this cause, we are all connected with the common thread of wanting to make the world a better place. Just think of all of the people you personally know who want to make the world a better place — your parents, your family doctor, the leader of your spiritual and/or religious group, your local humane society, the volunteers in your local community, etc. And now think of all of the organizations around the world whose sole purpose it is to make the world a better place by standing up for social justice, animal rights, human rights, or environmental protection. It's quite exciting, isn't it? All of these people, working and volunteering to make the world a better place, often at a personal sacrifice.

So my question to you is this: If so many individuals and organizations are dedicating their free time, careers, or even lives to making the world a better place, why do we still not live in peace and freedom? It doesn't make sense, does it? Shouldn't this common thread of wanting to make the world a peaceful place lead to common solutions for our global issues? And if the solutions were identified, would you be willing to make the sacrifices necessary to make them happen?

That last question is the hardest one. A good analogy can be taken from the movie The Matrix. In the film, the lead character Neo is given a choice of two pills. The blue pill allows him to go to sleep and wake up the next morning believing whatever he likes. The red pill allows him to see the truth. As Neo's mentor Morpheus says, "You have to see it for yourself. After this, there is no turning back. Remember, all I'm offering is the truth, nothing more."

Would you be willing to take a risk and swallow the red pill that shows you the truth? What if you learned that affecting positive change for global issues relating to social justice, animal rights, human rights, and the environment could be as simple as food choices? By adopting a plant-based, vegan diet, we can have a profound effect in all of these areas. Vegan benefits are felt most immediately in our state of health but extend well beyond into improving the global issues that affect us all. As Will Tuttle, Ph. D., and author of The World Peace Diet states, "Mindful eating is the essential foundation of happiness and peace."

WHAT IS VEGANISM?

To understand the potential global impact of veganism, we should start with the definition of that term. Although the practice of veganism has been noted throughout history, the founder of the Vegan Society, Donald Watson, defined the term "vegan" in 1944 as we understand and use it today. In coining the word, he distinguished vegan beliefs and habits from those of vegetarians. Generally, vegetarians abstain from eating meat, whereas vegans reject meat and animal products in all forms. Not only do they not consume meat, dairy, eggs, or honey, true vegans do not use any clothing, accessories or objects made from an animal.

BODY, MIND, AND SPIRIT

The Body: Improved Physical Health

Before I delve into the far-reaching benefits of a vegan lifestyle, I will begin with the personal advantages it brings to individuals. It's easy to say a new lifestyle improves our body, mind and spirit, but our very nature compels us to seek proof, and rightly so. For years, both the medical and scientific communities have been working to provide data that backs up this claim.

Neal D. Barnard, M.D., renowned physician and president of the Physicians Committee for Responsible Medicine, provides some of the most recent data supporting this claim. Results from his clinical study showed health improved on all fronts for participants with a plant-based diet. According to his research, "People not only slim down, but also see their cholesterol levels plummet and their blood pressure fall. If they have diabetes, it typically improves and sometimes even disappears. Arthritis pains and migraines often vanish, and energy comes racing back. Sluggishness vanishes, and they look and feel radiant."

Those are amazing results, aren't they? The physical benefits of a vegan diet go even further than those addressed by Dr. Barnard. Studies also demonstrate a direct correlation between a meatless diet and a lower body mass index (BMI), which is a typical indicator of healthy weight and lack of fat on the body. The International Journal of Obesity reported a six-year study by scientists at the University of Oxford with 38,000 participants of varied eaters (vegetarians, vegans, meat-eaters and fish-eaters) and found vegans to have the lowest BMI by a significant margin.

This lower BMI translates into healthy weight loss. Eating vegan eliminates most of the unhealthy foods that tend to cause weight issues. Once you adopt a vegan lifestyle, you develop an affinity for new foods, and as your palate changes, so do your cravings. By making a wise choice for your body, you begin to feel more positive.

Another benefit that vegans find as a result of their lifestyle is improved energy levels. More and more professional athletes attest to this, and what better source is there than the people whose very careers depend on their energy and stamina? To name just a few, former Celtics player Robert Parish, famed World Series Champion Hank Aaron and gold medal Olympian Carl Lewis are all major advocates of the vegan lifestyle. Lewis says, "I've found that a person does not need protein from meat to be a successful athlete. In fact, my best year of track competition was the first year I ate a vegan diet. Moreover, by continuing to eat a vegan diet, my weight is under control, I like the way I look. (I know that sounds vain, but all of us want to like the way we look.) I enjoy eating more, and I feel great."

German strongman Patrik Baboumian is another successful career athlete following a vegan diet. At Toronto's 2013 Vegetarian Food Festival, he clearly disproved any belief that to be a strong athletic competitor you must consume quantities of meat when he carried a yoke weighing more than 1200 pounds across the stage.

Outside of maintaining a healthy weight, being vegan improves the body physically in other ways. Healthy skin is dependent on antioxidants like beta-carotene and vitamins A, C and E, which are found predominantly in fruits and vegetables. It follows naturally that vegans will receive an infusion of these as compared to non-vegans. The elimination of dairy plays a role as well. Many dairy-producing cattle are injected with the growth hormone IGF-1, which causes swelling, redness, and clogged pores in humans. Even ailments such as PMS, migraines, and allergies decrease significantly with a vegan lifestyle.

The Mind: Improved Mental Health

In a 2012 issue of Nutrition Journal, Bonnie Beezhold and Carol Johnson reported findings that being vegan definitively improves a person's mood. In their study, participants were divided into three groups: omnivores, fish-eaters and vegetarians. After two weeks, participants completed a "Profile of Mood States" questionnaire and a "Depression Anxiety and Stress Scale" questionnaire. What were the results? The vegetarian group showed significant improvements in their mood scores at the end of the two-week trial. The findings were of no surprise to researchers, who have long known that meat and poultry diets are high in arachidonic acid (omega 6), which is linked to clinical symptoms of depression.

It's important to note, however, that omega 6 is an essential fatty acid, meaning our body does not manufacture it but requires it for good health. To find a balanced omega intake, vegans turn to plant sources instead, such as walnuts, pecans, avocado, flaxseed oil and other plant oils. Not only do these omega sources recover any deficiency that not eating meat may cause, they are also the same sources of vitamins known to improve mood. In other words, you're not only removing dietary items known to cause depression, you're adding foods that have the benefit of improving mood – a double bonus!

The Spirit: Improved Emotional Health

The emotional benefits of a vegan lifestyle are closely tied to the physical benefits. The bottom line is this: if you don't feel well physically, you won't be happy. Constant aches and pains quickly turn good emotional health into general unhappiness. Who among us hasn't had this experience? A lifestyle with good health and nutrition at its core can't help but improve your mood. When you eat well, you feel well.

Veganism also provides an opportunity for us to achieve success. Making the transition is not without challenges, and doing so successfully leads to a sense of pride and self-satisfaction. Our emotional health is better when we have embraced something wholeheartedly, as you do when you properly adhere to a vegan lifestyle. Simply put, it feels good to improve yourself and to do good for animals too.

A new lifestyle means new friends as well: another boost for our emotional health. Having a passion for a cause helps us become more outgoing as we seek to share our knowledge and excitement. A good deed shared by many feels even better than a good deed managed alone.

BEYOND OURSELVES

Now that you know about the personal benefits of veganism, it's time to discuss what to many vegans is even more important: how a vegan lifestyle lets us look beyond ourselves to improve the world. Sound dramatic? It is! Just imagine that a change in your lifestyle can implement change for everyone!

The Environment

"The sixteen hundred dairies in California's Central Valley alone produce more waste than a city of 21 million people — that's more than the populations of London, New York and Chicago combined." — Gene Baur, co-founder and president of Farm Sanctuary.

In a report published by the Food and Agriculture Organization of the United Nations (FAO), we learn that meat production has quadrupled in the past 50 years. Today, farmed animals (animals raised for consumption such as cattle, pigs, chickens, ducks, turkeys, egg-laying hens and dairy cows) outnumber people by more than three to one. Initially, "21 million people," "quadrupled in the past 50 years" and "more than three to one" seem like insurmountable figures, don't they? They certainly don't come across as something to be dealt with in the day-to-day life of average people like us. The truth is, these figures are of great importance to each and every one of us, as they warn us of increased global warming, pollution, water scarcity, deforestation, land degradation, species extinction and world hunger.

Consider, for instance, the relationship between farmed animals and global warming. As most of us know, scientists have been studying the results and effects of global warming's rising temperatures, rising sea levels, melting icecaps and glaciers and shifting ocean currents and weather patterns for years. It's no surprise that they've determined global warming is one of the most serious environmental challenges we're facing. So how is the amount of farmed animals related to global warming? The fact is, farmed animals are responsible for 18 percent of the greenhouse gas emissions that contribute to global warming. Just think about that for a minute. If everyone were to adopt a vegan lifestyle, we would cut emissions by almost a fifth.

Another factor in the correlation between the high farmed-animal count and negative impacts on the environment is the amount of water used to maintain them. The organization People for the Ethical Treatment of Animals (PETA) reports that it takes more than 2,400 gallons of water to produce one pound of meat, while growing one pound of wheat only requires 25 gallons. Not only is animal farming a great drain on natural water supplies, it's a major source of water pollution as a result of the animal waste, antibiotics and hormones, chemicals from tanneries, fertilizers and pesticides and sediments from eroded pastures that are found in water run-off.

Expansion of farmed animal production is also a key element in deforestation. In Latin America, 70 percent of what was once forested land in the region is now used for pastures and feedcrops. Land once valued for creating oxygen, filtering pollutants and stabilizing the global climate has been turned over to the farmed-animal industry. The natural benefits of these forests are lost, and species native to them are rapidly becoming endangered or extinct. Stripping the planet's green spaces is literally affecting the chances of your survival.

Equally concerning is the potential for farmed animal populations to cause world hunger to worsen. As more and more societies become dependent on farmed animals for a significant portion of their diet, the demand for meat is growing too rapidly to keep up with. According to the World Watch Institute, if everyone received 25 percent of their needed daily calories from animal products, only 3.2 billion people would have enough food to eat. Let's suppose that figure were lowered by just 10 percent. In that case, 4.2 billion people would be sustained. That's over 1 billion people more! So just think of what the complete removal of all animal products could do. The entire world population, more than 6.3 billion people, would go to bed every night with a full stomach.

The Animals

According to FAO, more than 60 billion animals are killed every year whether for food or product consumption. This figure is absolutely staggering, and it doesn't even take into consideration the number of animals killed accidentally, whether by farm incident, losing a home to crop cultivation or for mere sport.

In Animal Liberation, author Peter Singer explains the reasoning behind animal rights. He states that the basic principle of equality does not require equal or identical treatment; it requires equal consideration. This is a sentiment shared by many vegans. The question is not whether animals can reason or speak or function at a higher learning level. An inability to state their cause doesn't mean they don't have one. The question, asserts Singer, is whether animals deserve to be free of suffering.

Other proponents of animal rights would point to the selective nature of our diet. Eating a dog would be viewed with disgust in any American home. But a pig? Not an issue. Why is that? In this instance we have two animal species – just two among thousands – that have an equal ability to feel pain, fright, frustration, and contentment. Yet even with their "equal" abilities as higher thinkers, we feel justified in considering one species worthy of our loving homes and one species worthy of being our dinner.

At one time, the term "humane meat" began to take root in the agriculture industry in hopes it would improve relations with animal rights advocates. It meant that eating meat and dairy was justified if the animals were raised in good conditions and not mistreated. That concept, never accepted by vegans, is now beginning to erode with the general population too. Increasingly, reports are published of continued animal cruelty, and secret recordings by nonprofits such as Mercy for Animals are providing the proof. When we see the evidence on video, it is much harder to forget at our next meal how the meat came to be upon our plates. It is also much easier to see the value of a vegan lifestyle beyond its health benefits.

Righting Social Injustices

The social injustice of meat, dairy, egg and honey consumption is a direct result of speciesism: the belief that being human is a valid reason for human animals to have greater rights than non-human animals. To illustrate this point, a vegan will justifiably ask: Isn't raising animals for consumption another form of slavery? Treating a living and responsive creature as an object whose sole purpose is to fulfill our needs…this is slavery in its purest form.

Gary Smith, co-founder of Evolutus, has remarked, "150 years ago, they would've thought you were absurd if you advocated for the end of slavery. 100 years ago, they would have laughed at you for suggesting that women should have the right to vote. Fifty years ago, they would've objected to the idea of African-Americans receiving equal rights under the law. Twenty-five years ago, they called you a pervert if you advocated for gay rights. They laugh at us now for suggesting that animal slavery be ended. Someday they won't be laughing."

What's most striking about this is not the list of victimized and oppressed. Mankind has suffered victimization since the beginning of its history. What's most impressive is that the groups Smith refers to were successful in achieving their goals, however far-reaching they seemed at the time. They advocated their cause with an unwavering commitment to succeed that yielded results once never dreamed possible and were rewarded with magnificent outcomes. In the case of animals, they have no voice to advocate their cause, so it is imperative that we feel compassion towards them. Vegans are the human "voice" of non-human animals. Perhaps Will Tuttle, Ph. D., author of The World Peace Diet, provided the most effective inspiration for dedicating ourselves to the vegan lifestyle when he said, "The light of the infinite spiritual source of all life shines in all creatures. By seeing and recognizing this light in others, we free both them and ourselves. This is love."

Spreading the message

As more and more information comes to light that evidences why a vegan lifestyle has such positive global ramifications, we now turn to sharing that message with others. Every time we turn on our laptop and connect to the Internet, we have the opportunity to educate others on the importance of veganism through various social media sites. We are now able to meet, support, and discuss with people from all over the world instead of being limited to our nearby communities. The Internet provides an opportunity for vegans to stand together through online petitions and fundraising too.

As convenient and effective as the Internet is, let's not forget personal, face-to-face communication. Open a dialogue with a stranger or include a stranger in a conversation you're having with a vegan. Volunteer in a vegan group whose mission is to spread the word. Great strides can be made by working together. Lead by example and model veganism for others. Many people believe they'll have to sacrifice too much of what they love if they become a vegan. Invite guests over and prepare a vegan meal to show them what the food is like, but don't stop there: send the recipes home with them if they're interested. That small effort on your part will go a long way. The small amount of time you save them in searching for a recipe might be enough to encourage them to try out a new vegan lifestyle.

It is important to share the reasons for a vegan lifestyle; it's also critical to use the right means for doing so. In *Why We Love Dogs, Eat Pigs, and*

Wear Cows, social psychologist Dr. Melanie Joy says, "Often, vegan advocates assume that a person's defensiveness is the result of selfishness or apathy, when in fact it is much more likely the result of systematic and intensive social conditioning." With this in mind, approach each person thoughtfully and carefully. Remember, you're asking people to turn their world upside down. Their scepticism is natural. A pushy, demanding, or righteous presentation of facts usually only ensures defensiveness, annoyance, and a pre-determination to not try something new. Using a compassionate, gentle approach will yield greater benefits by far.

LAYING DOWN OUR WEAPON

More than 50 years ago Mahatma Gandhi said, "The most violent weapon on earth is the table fork." Today, science is able to prove the truth in Gandhi's statement. The negative effects of consuming animal products surround us: our forests are being decimated, the climate is increasingly unstable and atrocities against animals are worsening. The good news is that it's not too late to stop the devastation. I said earlier in this chapter that the common thread binding humanity is its desire for harmony and peace.

It was also Gandhi who said, "Be the change you want to see in the world." Each and every one of us has the opportunity to be the change we want to see in the world through the choices we make. I choose to follow in Gandhi's footsteps by living a vegan lifestyle towards harmony and peace. What do you choose? Here, now, is your opportunity. It's as simple as living vegan. If we individually do our part as vegans, then collectively we will have taken massive strides toward achieving our goal for peace. Will you join me in changing the world?

To learn more about a vegan lifestyle, please visit my website at www.MrsGreenjeansPlantsSeeds.com/book, where you can get a free list of hidden animal ingredients in foods.

Break Through Your Barriers & Live Your Dreams

Sandra Westland

Every woman deserves to feel powerful and successful, and the opportunity to do so stands right before her. She doesn't have to be a warrior to smite every dragon or burn down every obstacle that stands in her way. She simply needs to connect with and be her real, authentic self. So her journey to success begins by standing still, by being curious about the world of potential that exists within her and in front of her, and by understanding her inner world in order to ignite change in her outer one towards her success.

But, what stops her from becoming the author of her own life, from being all she can be? The glass ceiling, the unofficial barrier that prevents women from rising up to executive positions or from running their successful businesses, does still exist. Yet, in my twenty-five years of education, hypno-psychotherapy and peak performance training, I see, more significantly, an individual's own inner glass ceiling capping and limiting the success in life that is there for the taking.

To be a woman is to be extraordinary. We all have it within us to move beyond an ordinary life and its everyday limitations to embrace our desires and possibilities, harness our untold natural potential and live the life we are meant to live —a life of personal freedom in which we simply are our natural, awesome selves. Your power is switched on when you embrace, embody, express and enjoy being a woman. Your energy is released when you learn to live truly in your own skin. I love being a woman, and I love continuing to find out just what that is like for me.

This is a journey of discovering your place in life as a woman and as a woman in business, a voyage into your inner mind's processing and the terrain of your inner world, deeper than your conscious mind can be aware of. It is an expedition through self-alignment, forming the detail of your desired outcomes, shaping your life to fit with your passions, sourcing the energy that drives you, thus smashing your glass ceiling and allowing your transformation to unfold. Just as I experienced my own first steps, I want you also to stride out along this path and the journey of becoming your potential. The message I write within the pages of *Smashing Your Glass Ceiling* takes you through this fascinating journey where "Wow, I didn't realize that" and "No wonder I wasn't getting to where I wanted to" are familiar insights.

HOW DOES IT ALL WORK?

The tools you will need for such a journey of self-discovery are drawn from Neuro-Linguistic Programming (NLP), guided imagery, and a gentle questing into uncovering your own uniqueness and meaning in life. In blending these time-tested methods into one programme, it's possible to break through all that's holding you back in life.

From my own personal experience as a woman and as a psychotherapist and trainer, I've found that one of the most powerful tools we naturally have and need to embrace first is the power of imagination; even if you think you have one or not, you really do have an amazing, creative imagination. It just may need awakening and a little encouraging. I would love to show you just how powerful your imagination can be and how crucial it is to connect with you and be your own woman. In beginning this imaginative journey, you are sparking off a chain of events that produce fundamental changes in your physical body, starting with the neurological processes that will link to your biology and produce within you "decision states" leading to the different outcomes that you want, easily and naturally. Imagine the decisions that you can make or the actions that you can take when you are feeling confident, in balance and aligned to your vision, compared to the choices that you opt for when you are upset, anxious, depressed and out of sync with yourself.

By guiding your imagination, you can form an internal vision in which you are taking the right path for you to succeed in your life, and then formulate just what that is. As you immerse yourself in the excitement and the thrill of being on the right road to greatness, you tap into the inner confidence and self-reliance, inner freedom and success awareness that generate your momentum to smashing your glass ceiling. The power is always within you. It's just a case of summoning and connecting with it.

Imagine also gaining new understanding into how you process information from your "now" experiences, how you view the world, how you communicate with others and how they communicate with you. Imagine how much easier your life would be. You can learn how to recognize ways of processing external data and how, by modifying your communication in a way that makes sense to others, your relationships become infinitely warmer, richer and more connected.

Think about meeting me in the flesh for the first time, already knowing how my inner world works. Wouldn't it be good to know I'm an auditory person? Why? Well, my world is very much filtered through sounds. I will be finely tuned into noise ... all noise. I will get distracted with too much of it, and I will recognize very slight changes in your voice, tone and pitch. So I will hear a hint of doubt or an emotion rising from within you just by hearing your voice. If you speak too slowly or very loudly, this will create a dissonance within me. If you use language that talks about "viewing something" or "seeing what you mean" or "having a handle on this or that" instead of "sounds like" or "listen to", I will feel a mismatch between us. Don't click your pen or tap it on the table if you want me to be relaxed! It's only a slight inner discomfort, but it undeniably shapes how I experience you and your communication. Upon our meeting, if you appreciate my world and I appreciate yours, we will hit it off with ease. I will look to communicate to you through your world, which may be visual, auditory, kinesthetic or auditory digital, all very different ways of experiencing and processing, and you can do the same for me.

GETTING TO KNOW YOUR GLASS CEILING

Your internal glass ceiling may have been created from prejudgments, prejudices, cultural and social attitudes that operate deep within the unconscious, taken in when young. So, it's crucial to find these out and know how they work for you, to understand the inner conflicts that are holding you back and what they mean. In speaking with a senior executive upon her reading *Smashing Your Glass Ceiling*, she'd suddenly become aware of how she was dressing like a man for her banking boardroom meetings. It wasn't her at all, but after further exploration, she realized she had unconsciously thought it would help men relate to her and allow her to be "taken seriously". She was shocked at how unconscious this had been, but she was relieved to learn it and is now enjoying the fun of finding out who she is as a woman in business and what clothes this exploration leads her to wearing. It is only by excavating these unconscious gender biases and other judgments that contribute towards making your own ceiling that you can reveal your real, natural self to yourself and the world. In understanding yourself more and knowing just who you are and how you are in the world, you become free to choose how to respond to situations and to people, and then you really begin to own your own life.

I am wondering just what you are thinking, having read these thousand plus words. Is this possible for you or is your glass ceiling giving you bother, preventing you from imagining and thinking of all that you can be? What does your ceiling hold and what is it whispering to you right now? What is your "default" setting?

Are you someone who assumes you won't find a car parking space and prove yourself right, or do you simply know that it doesn't matter where you park and thus usually find one just when and where you need it? Is a potential redundancy at work a chance to do something different, or a terrible catastrophe that you will never escape? Your attitudes play a massive part in your life experiences, and to how much you can grow. Zig Ziglar's famous saying "Your attitude determines your altitude" is so true. So, how do your attitudes determine how successful you can be?

I have lived and refined through my own personal journey a framework of all the things that are crucial to help you aspire to be. Let's make a start right now, something to get you thinking. Let's peek into those achieving just what you want and begin to emulate some of what they do and how they are. It's as good a place as any to start!

In NLP terms, this is called "modeling". In modeling the behaviors and habits of successful people, we're seeking to learn from successful businesswomen and successful women just what it is that they do, and what it is that they have that makes them successful; not to become them, but to incorporate their winning behaviours into our repertoire, choosing those which are congruent with us and amplifying them. I often explore other women that I admire and am drawn to. In carefully watching what they do and exploring this within my own life, in my way, I can open up to further resources that I naturally have, but have yet to connect with. In Sue Knight's' words, "If you spot it, you've got it." (NLP at Work, 2013)

Now to stoke up those neurological pathways as we vamp it up a little more and transport you forward into your own fabulous future. Familiarize yourself with the state of being successful with no glass ceiling, as if you've already accomplished that level of success, a dress rehearsal if you like. Put on the mantle of success and ask yourself how and what do you feel, how would your day evolve, what can you do now that you couldn't do before. How would others perceive you? Get your brain to make it a done deal so that it can look for it, search it out and create it. This is the self-fulfilling prophecy at its most positive, potent and powerful.

Anticipate now becoming friendly and familiar with a future you who has everything you need and want and to be able to use the guidance of that future you – the answers may very well surprise you. My future self enlightened me as to my fear of success! This helped me find my inner glass ceiling and the meaning of it all, so I could smash it and really begin to find out just what I could do and what was possible in life. I believe that to guide others you have to have lived the journey yourself, and so my own personal journey has and is this path too, encompassing where I am finding myself … as a woman, an educator, therapist and businesswoman. This is a journey I don't ever intend to stop.

PEELING BACK THE ONION

There is so much more to explore! As humans, we've infinite depths, so exploring your inner beliefs, your values and mission is crucial for success. It's the peeling back of the onion, layer by layer (corny, I know), but I assure you that the exploration, while deep, is richly rewarding. Wouldn't you rather know what's holding you back and why you may feel frustrated with yourself? I know I would. I simply want to make the most of my time on this earth and experience it as much as possible. Life is to be lived and not simply endured and got through.

Excavate your inner beliefs, isolate the limiting ones that have held you back, and then you will easily and naturally begin to fly! Once figured out, you become empowered as you re-think and re-frame beliefs into being resourceful, productive and desirable, and turn them into second nature.

Let's go one deeper. Do you know just what it is that you value, all those things that are really important to you? Are they aligned with your life? These are your GPS, and if you're frustrated, feel trapped in the mundane of life or have unwanted physical/emotional symptoms, then value fine-tuning is needed for you to move forward in the direction that you want to go. Let's not be sidetracked by detours, road closures and an unclear destination. Being authentic and all that you are needs you to know what you value so that you're able to craft your mission for the ultimate alignment. In *Smashing Your Glass Ceiling* or my Success workshops , you will not short-change yourself here. I will journey with you, helping you along the way through a process of simple, yet profoundly powerful steps.

When you are fully aligned, there will be no holding you back. You'll meet the right person at the right time, and you'll have the right skills to achieve your goals. Everything will fall into place like a jigsaw puzzle, and you'll have "the strength, the patience, and the passion to reach for the stars", to borrow the words of a courageously inspiring woman, Harriet Tubman.

LOADING UP ON INTERNAL RESOURCES

It's not all plain sailing, and you *will* be derailed by the unexpected, but what makes someone a success is their ability to keep going, even when challenged. So, one of the final steps in the Programme is to load you up with the internal resources to get you through when things get sticky, and when, quite frankly, you wonder why you bother. NLP strategies reprogram how we react and respond to such times, making a monumental difference to how you experience your life. If you're feeling down on yourself, I will show you that you can change your physiology. If you're getting increasingly anxious about an upcoming meeting, you can change your self-talk, the inner conversation you're having with yourself, to something more upbeat, more encouraging and more positive.

Powerful NLP strategies are there for you to use at any time and in any situation. Your life will be richer and filled with more options when you are able to redirect your thinking and focus, stay resourceful in stressful situations, and generate behaviors and outcomes that are positive for you and your life.

Finally, if this chapter has inspired you to delve deeper into Smashing your Glass Ceiling, the book comes with a number of bonuses, some of which can be downloaded from my website, www.SmashingYourGlassCeiling.com for you to enjoy absolutely free. So, get started now and embrace the fact that you are an extraordinary woman.

TAKING THE FIRST STEP

All of us have to start somewhere. I did when I was thirty-four, when I found myself looking at twenty-six more years before retirement, counting the years and the days till the next school holiday. Not how I imagined my life would be.

By becoming curious, asking questions of myself and tapping into effective life-changing techniques that opened me up to the power and potential of the mind, I'm on a fascinating journey. I'm continuing to smash my own internal glass ceiling, and am living out my passion to enhance the lives of other women. I am certainly not "sorted out", nor have I "self-actualized" and not every day is "grrreat", but I know that every day is an adventure with the chance to grow further and find out more about just what is possible.

The more women I meet and work with, the more I learn and the more I gather evidence to support my belief that, as women, we owe it to ourselves to be extraordinary. This is my invitation to you to take the first steps with me on your own journey of becoming all you wish to be.

Sandra Westland is an experienced educator, therapist and successful businesswoman who helps others to find their passion and fulfil their dreams. She has a Master's degree in Existential Psychotherapy, an Education Honours degree, and is a practicing Advanced Hypnotherapist and NLP practitioner. Her doctoral thesis explores women and their relationship with their bodies. She is the author of Smash Your Glass Ceiling and co-author of Thinking Therapeutically.

Sandra is a Director of the Contemporary College of Therapeutic Studies, where she trains people at life changing junctures to be aspiring therapists, so they too can enjoy the enriching privilege of helping others to find their path in life. She is also a co-founder of Self Help School™, which provides psycho-education for the public and is an international speaker on the power of the mind for change.

www.ingramcontent.com/pod-product-compliance
Lightning Source LLC
Chambersburg PA
CBHW070803100426
42742CB00012B/2229